Community Water Management

Community Water Management

G.S. Narwani

RAWAT PUBLICATIONS
Jaipur and New Delhi

ISBN 81-7033-913-8

Published by
Prem Rawat for *Rawat Publications*
Satyam Apts., Sector 3, Jawahar Nagar, Jaipur 302 004 (India)
Phone: 0141 265 1748 / 7006 Fax: 0141 265 1748
E-mail: info@rawatbooks.com
Website: www.rawatbooks.com

Delhi Office
4858/24, Ansari Road, Daryaganj, New Delhi 110 002
Phone: 011-23263290

Typeset by Rawat Computers, Jaipur
Printed at Chaman Enterprises, New Delhi

Contents

Preface

Water is lifeblood of the community. It is a gift of nature to humankind since times immemorial. In ancient times community settlements were established on the river banks where water could be easily available for sustenance of humans, animals as well as plants. But, gradually, when kingdoms were established, laws were made, and management of water resources also became a state subject. In the post-independence period, with the big irrigation projects coming up in India to usher in green revolution in the country, community becomes water receiver and the state becomes water supplier for which maintenance charges are levied on the community. Farmers as water users are interested to get water for their fields in a fairly reliable way with more concern for sufficiency than with efficiency.

By and large, farmers become more knowledgeable and are interested in raising returns from land. They have become productivity-oriented now. They complain if water does not reach the tail end and their crops are spoiled. This consciousness as water users has raised demand for participatory management of water resources. With more knowledge about soils, pests, land practices, optimum use of water and other inputs draws greater attention and case for community participation became much stronger.

Due to decline in fiscal capability as a result of mounting operation and maintenance costs and inability to satisfy increasing number of complaints from water users, state agency now prefers to become 'wholesaler' rather than 'retailer' of water to create an enabling environment in society. New water policy also envisages privatization of water resources. But, the state is still interested in exercising control over water indirectly through water users and private agencies, though there is worldwide trend of devolution of natural resources to community.

Recently, governments have also started the practice of privatization of drinking water in favour of multinational companies after pressure from the World Bank. It has given rise to people's movement because monopoly of private companies is likely to exploit the water users by charging higher rates for water supply. Case of Vivendi company of France is a recent example. This company has raised the water charges from 24 paise to 59 paise in few years and invested funds out of government loans. It had to run away due to hue and cry from the community.

Rajendra Singh, the Magsaysay award winner, under the banner of 'National Water Brotherhood' organized India-wide rallies from 30 January 2003 to create awareness in the community against privatization of water and propagate for change in water policy so that water is treated as joint property of the government and the community.

The National Water Conference, organized at Sewa Gram, also oppose the 'National Water Policy' of the Government of India regarding commercialization of water resource given by nature. The government was warned not to play with fundamental and birth right of people over water.

Panchayats of Kerala have even gone to the extent of organizing 'World Water Conference' from 21 January 2004 and 'battle for water' is being fought between people and

Coco-Cola company against overexploitation of groundwater. Pepsi-Cola is another target. Villagers, mostly Dalits and tribals, are struggling for their right to water. The struggle at Plachimada (Kerala) is part of the worldwide struggle against transnational companies that exploit natural resources like water. Thus, resistance against stealing of water from the common man is being globalized. The '*Plachimada Declaration*' adopted at the end of the conference emphasized that "water is not a private property, not a commodity, but a common resource, a fundamental right of man. The right to conserve, use and manage water is fully vested with local community. This is the very basis of water democracy. Any attempt to reduce or deny this right is a crime". It is in this background that the whole issue of community management of water has to be viewed now.

In view of battle of community for water, this book traces the attempts of community participation in management of water resources through irrigation tanks, lift irrigation projects, irrigation tubewells, water harvesting structures in watershed development projects, groundwater resources, multipurpose irrigation projects and the Swajaldhara schemes under Rajiv Gandhi Drinking Water Mission.

I am thankful to Shri Kailashji of Rawat Publications, who was source of inspiration to me for writing on this subject of current interest and publishing it within a short time in an attractive form.

G.S. Narwani

1

WATER RESOURCES IN COMMUNITY LIFE

Clean air to breathe, safe water to drink and healthy food to eat are the bare minimum necessities of life. Every society has to give priority to provision these amenities for all its people. Nature has been kind to give us the resources needed to provide these basic amenities to all Indians. Everything that is essential for life is available in great abundance on the earth. Living creatures need air in order to breathe and air is plentiful. They must drink water and numerous sources of drinkable water-streams, springs, ponds, etc., exist. They must eat food. Food comes from plants, and plants are abundant over large areas of land. This easy availability of air, water and plants has brought about the proliferation of life that we see around us. The three main necessities of life, air, water and plants, are found in abundance on earth but not in infinite quantity. However, we have not succeeded in harnessing these resources properly through sound planning, careful upkeep and judicious management.

Without water, there can be no plants and without plants, no food and therefore no life. We thus see that water is essential not only for supporting life on the earth but also for its very existence. Bodies of plants and animals are full of water. About

70 per cent weight of human body is water. Blood is largely water. There is water inside and outside every cell. Water and soil are considered a boon of nature to mankind. Land as a resource cannot possibly be considered as a resource in isolation from water. Water is a crucial environmental resource for sustenance of life and economic well-being. It is on water that human, animal and plant life thrives on this planet. Thus *Water sustains life.* It is the most precious national resource both for survival and development, specially in view of rise in human and livestock population putting increasingly greater pressure on land and water resources.

That is why, the great old civilizations all over the world have flourished on river banks where land became productive by river waters.

River Nile – Egyptian civilization
River Indus and Ganga – Indian civilization
River Hwang-Ho – Chinese civilization

In many regions of the earth, there is no problem about the availability of water. Where there is substantial and frequent rainfall, there is usually enough water in the soil and we see a luxuriant growth of plants and trees. But in certain regions, such as deserts and hilly regions, where rainfall is scanty and there is little moisture in the soil, plants are scarce and so are living creatures. Occasionally, rainfall eludes even those areas which usually have sufficient rain. When this happens, the soil becomes dry, plants wither and there is a shortage of food and drinking water. Human beings have learnt to draw hidden water from underground in such situations.

Even in the Himalayas where water flows in abundance, it is a fact that due to seasonality of precipitation and inadequate water storage capacities, most of the river water flows down to the plains and then to the sea. Only a small proportion of available water is harnessed for productive and consumption purposes. Water is renewable but a limited resource made available through a complex hydrological cycle comprising of a set of related ecological processes. Water is made available to the eco-system through precipitation, surface run off, replenishing of groundwater and is finally returned to the atmosphere through evaporation and transpiration. Water has many competitive uses. It is required for agriculture, forestry, horticulture, for biomass growth, for industry, for drinking, for domestic uses, for animals and for a host of other purposes. The development of the population away from water resources has suffered scarcity and misery of famine and drought.

Man cannot live without bread. Bread comes from crops. Crops are raised through water only. Hence man has to eat what water and soil can produce. Nearly 80 per cent of water is used for raising crops. All development plans in any command area can be formulated with the help of either irrigation or management of water. No development is possible without sufficient water supply. Therefore, the modern civilization has to befriend rivers and use them for their development specially in under-developed countries like India.

Scarcity of Water

Management of water has to be an important focus of any protective and regenerative strategy. In India, 70 per cent of the cultivated area lies in the region of medium and low rainfall. Further, India utilizes only 28 per cent of rain water and 72 per cent flows away in rivers and nallahs. Though water is most essential resource for agriculture, it has to be conserved for development of agriculture which is the main source of livelihood in developing countries like India.

Scarcity of water has arisen mainly due to scanty rainfall, lack of conservation of rain water, excessive use of water in crop irrigation and maximum withdrawal of groundwater without equivalent recharge of water. Water is a valuable gift of nature to mankind but it is not to be squandered away. Every drop of it is valuable. If water flows waste or is utilized excessively without care, future generations will curse us for scarcity of water. If water resources are utilized carefully, they can last longer for our progeny.

UNO has already predicted that 21st century will witness battles on account of either terrorism or water. At the level of nations, numerous conflicts over river waters continue to pose a threat to peace and stability in several parts of the third world. If we analyze the situation in India, the picture is not different. The dispute about Cauvery waters between Tamil Nadu and Karnataka has gone up to the Supreme Court of India and revolts have started on account of it. Distribution of river waters is a bone of contention between Uttar Pradesh and Rajasthan over Yamuna waters and Punjab and Rajasthan over Sutlej river water which reaches Rajasthan Canal. Sardar Sarovar issue between the states of Gujarat, Rajasthan, Madhya Pradesh and Maharashtra is still alive.

Management of Water Resources

The World Bank Report on 'Water Resources Management' has discussed its crucial dimensions. Over the past two decades, it has pointed out to basic weaknesses as under:

1. A fragmented and often incoherent institutional approach to water management;
2. An overemphasis on new investment programmes combined with limited attention to ensuring effective administration, operation and maintenance (A, O & M) of existing infrastructure;
3. Poor integration of environmental considerations; and
4. Allocation of resources on an ad hoc basis rather than in accordance with sound priorities identified through assessments of benefits and costs or through explicit schemes aiming to privilege the poor.

Combination of centralized and decentralized management of water resources – uneven development – larger sums have been invested in hydro and irrigation management while poor and remote populations are neglected or remain unserved. Costs of supplying water in drought prone areas during emergencies are substantial.

Crucial Dimensions

- Water is not a scarce resource in most river basins in normal and wet years. Total quantity of water available is sufficient to meet demands from agriculture, electricity, industrial and residential sectors as well as to protect environmental resources. But time profile of demands over the seasons may not be consistent with preserving adequate flows for downstream users and environmental protection.
- Water rights must be viewed as being contingent on the amount of rainfall during the rainy season.
- Location is a third dimension which is not adequately represented in the way water rights are managed. Access to water for irrigation must ensure redistribution for poor beneficiaries. Conflict over water rights is a natural corollary of above dimensions.

Ways Forward

- Water infrastructure is managed by competent specialist enterprises who may collect charges from water users.
- Radical decentralization of responsibility for operation and management, giving a substantial role to local user associations or similar organizations (looking to success in irrigation sector) charges directly linked to expenditure on operative maintenance.

The success will of course depend on commitment of both the users and those responsible for the infrastructure. Users should be homogenous and well organized. Diversity of interests among the users will greatly increase the difficulties of agreeing on priorities. Though community management approach is not a universal palliative and it is definitely open to the charge of discrimination against small farmers and other poor water users, but the community arrangements tend to benefit large number of water users. However, a balanced approach based on proper evaluation of benefits and potential dangers is essential.

Population Explosion

These conflicts have intensified in recent years over natural resources in many parts of the Third World. Main reason has been that development measures have not kept pace with population growth. Competing demands on the same resources of land, water and biomass by different people result in protracted conflicts, sometimes of a violent nature. These scales unfold at various scales from individuals to nation-states. At the individual level, conflicts over plots of land under uncertain or changing land tenure are widespread. These conflicts demonstrate the lack of sustainability of natural resource management. In such context, conservation, management and development of natural resources on a scientific basis is essential to ensure a sustainable development process. A healthy conjunction between man and nature is essential for the success of developmental planning. Our land is finite but being burdened with pressure of ever increasing population, we need to develop areas and location specific land and water management practices. Enormous rise in human population and the same increase in bovine population has put tremendous pressure on landmass. This has not only resulted in reduction of per capita availability of net area cultivated but also a substantial reduction in availability of common properties for grazing and fuel wood for the cattle population and village community respectively.

Management of Natural Resources

There have also been cases of grabbing of common property by some influential groups of villagers. In earlier years, the pressure on land was not so much, hence nobody thought of management of common property lands. Today the situation is different. Demands of ever increasing population has raised demand for fuel, fodder and food grains. There is a big question mark regarding government management of lands, forests and water resources. Hence, serious effort is essential so that management of natural resources meets the basic requirements of people on an equitable basis without causing environmental damage.

Both the Forest Conservation Act, 1980 and the Indian Forest Act, 1927 provided for management of common property resources. Article 39 (B) of the Constitution of India provides that the control of material resources of the community are so distributed so as to best subserve the common good. Both National Forest Policy, 1988 and the National Water Policy, 1987 have also acknowledged the importance of common property resources and common lands.

The National Water Policy, 1987 mentions that "economic development and activities including agriculture, industrial and urban development should be planned with due regard to constraints imposed by configuration of water availability. There should be a water zoning of the country and economic activities should be guided and regulated in accordance with such zoning".

The National Forest Policy, 1988 also stressed that "village and community lands including those on foreshores and environs of tanks not required for other productive uses should be taken up for development of tree crops and fodder resources..."

Similarly, the Technical Committee on Drought Prone Area Programme and Desert Development Programme (1994), while recommending development on watershed basis, also opined that "since the objective of watershed development is ecological improvement and conservation of natural resources as well as socio-economic development of local population, watershed management efforts must incorporate soil and water conservation and land use planning into a broader framework that takes into consideration not only physical interrelationship but economic, social and institutional factors as well... Appropriate arrangements should be made for distribution of benefits to watershed community from the government lands and watershed development".

Equal Rights of all Sections of the Community

Common property resources like village pastures, community forests, village tanks, waste lands, waste dumping places, watershed drainage, rivers and rivulets, riverbeds and even groundwater are resources accessible to the whole community. Every individual has equal right to share its benefit and there are even legal provisions to such effect. But it is observed in practice that some influential persons monopolize the benefits and the interest of poor is sacrificed. The voice of the poor remains unheard or it is a voice in wilderness. Hence, efficient land and water management is of crucial importance in the face of land and water being limited in supply and claimants of land and water being numerous. With liberalized economic policy and competitive economic development, the management of natural resources is at stake.

Participative Management by the Community

Hence, the Government of India, in plan document 1992-97, acknowledged that "developmental activities undertaken with people's active participation have greater chances of success... The role of the government should be to facilitate the process of people's involvement in developmental activities by creating the right type of institutional infrastructure, primarily in rural areas".

We cannot live without nature but its resources are not unlimited. Hence, we cannot extract them beyond certain limits. A constant extracting process of natural resources has caused their depletion which has polluted not only the environment but has also upset the ecological balance in the biosphere. The environment and ecological problems arising out of depletion of natural resources are not specific only to a country or nation but to the whole globe. Hence, immediate measures are needed for preservation, management and development of natural resources.

Natural resources cannot be managed and preserved properly without involving rural communities which derive their sustenance from natural resources. Role of communities is to manage natural resources in an optimum manner. Participation of people in shaping their destiny is the essence of democratic governance. People can understand their best interest and specially guard against interest of the poor provided they keep the community really in the forefront. People-centred and people-managed paradigm of development has been gaining popularity in recent years. In view of the changing scenario at global, national and regional levels, development must now be radically reviewed. It must be around people and not people around development. It should empower people in view of democracy as a prevailing system of governance.

Participative management of natural resources is not a sudden development. It has a long history. Chinese educator Jimmi Yen advocated following principles for large-scale people's participation in China sometimes in mid-forties:

- Go to people
- Live with them
- Learn from them
- Serve them
- Love them
- Plan with them
- Start with what they know
- Build on what they have

These are really the basic principles to seek people's willing cooperation and real participation in all programmes relating to conservation, management and development of natural resources. People's potential will, of course, has to be developed by increasing their capacity and capabilities through education, training and continuous participation at all stages of planning and execution.

In the above context, people-centred and people-controlled paradigm of development has acquired new urgency in present times. In view of changing scenario at global, national and regional level, development must now be radically reviewed and revised. It must be woven around people who should be empowered. The World Development Report (1992) opined that projects are more successful if they are participatory in design and implementation. Involvement of people in a project at all levels gives them a sense of ownership which in turn makes them accountable.

People's participation presumes following features:

— Centrality of people is the essence of participation. Any programme should be based on felt needs of people.

— People themselves should analyze their condition and propose the project.

— Capacity building should be done to develop local capacity and mobilize local resources. People's potential can be increased by improving their capabilities through education, training and participation in developmental activities.

— Indigenous technical knowledge, technique and local methods should be valued.

— Marginalized classes must be associated and encouraged to participate actively.

— Women should also be included as equal partners.

— People should be taken into confidence that they are real planners, and benefits will also accrue to them in short run and long run.

— People must be associated in execution and monitoring also.

The natural resources are a boon of nature to mankind, but they had been controlled by the state government departments of revenue, forest, irrigation, fisheries, public health engineering, etc., for earning revenues for the State and were badly managed in the past. Poor people were denied its benefits which were monopolized by few landlords, big farmers, contractors, industrialists and influential sections of society. Hence, now it is high time to vest back these natural resources to the people themselves through Gram Sabha or user committees for proper management, preservation and development to the optimum possible extent and to the best interest of the community as a whole, including poor and marginalized classes.

References

Edwards, Michael and Alan Fowler (eds.), *The Earthscan Reader on NGO Management*, Earthscan, London, 2002.

Hooja, Rakesh, Ganesh Pangare and K.V. Raju, *Users in Water Management*, Rawat Publications, Jaipur, 2002.

Joshi, L.K. and Rakesh Hooja (eds.), *Participatory Irrigation Management*, Rawat Publications, Jaipur, 2000.

Mishra, G.P. and B.K. Bajpai (eds.), *Community Participation in Natural Resource Management*, Rawat Publications, Jaipur, 2001.

Sharma, B.D., *The People Versus The System*, Sahyog Pustak Kutir, New Delhi, 1998.

World Bank, "Water Resources Management", *Project Report*, 17541.

2

Management of Water Resources in Retrospect

After World War II, when development processes started, governments were basically responsible for it in developed as well as developing countries. For dealing with problems of rural development, water and sanitation, health and education, environment and forests, agriculture and employment, tribal welfare, women welfare, etc., mainly government ministries, departments and other agencies were responsible. Though there is full-fledged democracy in India and democratic decentralization has also remained in practice since 1959, participation of people at grassroots is still a distant dream. Even after provision of holding and empowering Gram Sabhas in the Constitution of India through 73rd Constitution Amendment 1993, active involvement and empowerment of women, Scheduled Castes and Scheduled Tribes is yet to be fully achieved. The community does not like to actively involve itself in the management of even social services directly affecting their living like education, health, woman and child development, drinking water and the like. Why is it so?

The changing role of the state in development, during the first three quarters of 20th century, can be seen as one where states held clear authority within their borders, acquired growing functions and tended to perform them on their own. The latter part of the 20th century and the beginning of 21st century witnessed a more porous view of the nation-state, fewer directly performed functions and more partnership with other actors. In countries which became independent after World War II, states filled the post-colonial 'vacuum' as a matter of policy transfer. Aid agencies for agricultural and industrial projects wanted state guarantees. Idea of state-led development was attractive. It apparently offered a way of satisfying popular expectations and demonstrating a concern for social justice and development.

The case for state-led development was not only imitative but also built on a response to local circumstances. Where market institutions were weak and state enterprises were capable of investing, development and welfare became duty of the state.

Criticisms of State Activism in Developing Countries

1. State could run public administration only and could not become an agent of development. Bureaucracy was biased towards stability. They were anti-developmental and suppressed entrepreneurial interests. Public sector often served particular interests.
2. 'Softness' and 'weakness' of the state. It does not have capacity to enforce policy.
3. Bureaucracy was subordinated to non-national interests. Far from being the agent of development, the state was seen as an agent of underdevelopment or distorted development.
4. By the end of 1970s, with international recession, growing national debt in Latin America and Africa, and widespread military regimes, there was deep pessimism about the scope for development and scepticism about the state's role.

Where are we now?

The last decade of the 20th century and the first decade of the 21st century have seen a shift from simple commitment to market liberalization. Free markets and liberal economic policies are seen now to be important but not enough on their own. Conditions are to be created in which citizens and markets can flourish. These conditions include clear property rights, the rule of law, financial systems, active civil society, good government and effective public administration. Government and public administration will perform their own direct functions but they will also interact and support private and community actors. There is also wide recognition of the importance of rule-based professional bureaucracy to provide the basic services and honest dealings in which business and citizens can flourish.

The People versus the System

As the state fails to direct the process of change in India and surrenders before the global neo-imperialist-capitalist axis under the garb of so-called liberalization and globalization, the development itself has assumed a stark anti-people stance. The people specially in rural areas are considered as ignorant, inexperienced, non-technical, prone to corruption as if bureaucrats are the only technical, knowledgeable and experienced lot. Local people have been performing miracles with lime and mortar which civil engineers failed to achieve with iron and steel as far as durability of assets is concerned. Indigenous technological knowledge has been widely recognized the world over.

But people can no more be ignored as they have realized the power of their vote and their right to change rulers. The people's movements, in the face of new challenge, have added a new dimension to the state-sponsored and market-centred processes of change and development. They insist, in their own idiom and style, which is not as yet fully understood by rulers – that the change and development should be people-centred.

Historical Perspective

Centralization of authority and counter-assertion by the people has been an incessant process ever since the dawn of civilization. There were, however, limits to centralization on account of logistics of control, the unpredictable human factor involved at all levels in the chain of command, the possibility of even smaller groups asserting in respective territorial units and ubiquitous emergence of leaders of resistance. This situation continued some 300 years ago when a qualitative change occurred in the wake of industrial revolution, which expanded the span of control of institutions dramatically.

A phase of transformation occurred after 'renaissance'. There was a breakthrough in scientific discoveries and their use for technological innovations. It culminated in the great industrial revolution and ushered in the capitalistic phase in the production system. Man acquired a new source of power with almost unlimited scope. The expanding production capacity became an instrument for territorial expansion and it laid the foundations of imperialist-capitalist global hegemony. Resources and also the people in the occupied territories were to serve as the base for colonial masters. The 'white man' created an aura for himself as if he was "carrying the cross of civilizing the world" and called it white man's burden. Imperial powers created a new class which according to Macaulay would be "English in spirit and Indians in colour and form". They proved successful in this mission. The new elite has been drawing their inspiration from the imperialist world and consequently the process of change has been largely external. The new divide has assumed broadly the form of 'urban-organized' versus 'rural-unorganized'.

The expansion of centralized control took two forms. There was greater consolidation of groups nearer the centre of authority, sharing similar characteristics. Secondly, the hitherto unchartered territories could also be brought under more effective centralized authority in contrast with loose formations earlier. The concurrent advancement on the economic front generated larger dividends, which were shared more equitably at home, notwithstanding the capitalistic exploitation. A bitter struggle followed among the imperialist powers for control over the globe, which continued till about the middle of the 20th century. The world, during this imperial phase, was formally divided into two 'worlds'. The people in the colonies had no place in this frame, not being recognized even as human beings worthy of any consideration. Imperialism progressed with the divine dictate of white man's burden. It was driven by nascent capitalist engines of power.

The mid-20th century witnessed the dismantling of the formal imperial structures. The erstwhile colonial territories acquired status of independent countries. The change, or artificial definition of their physical boundaries has led to a lot of confusion after independence. The major issue, in many cases, remained assertion of national identity even after long periods of apparent consensus about the larger identity, as in the case of Yogaslavia and Pakistan or fractured identities as in the case of Hongkong, Taiwan or even the German states.

The erstwhile colonial nation-states adopted generally the political system of their master nations. All these systems, by their very nature, had the colonial mould. The internecine warfare amongst various interest groups, in the name of democratic institutions, led to their supersession by the most powerful element in the structure, that is, military dictators in most cases. In some cases, as in Cuba, dictatorship of proletariat overwhelmed. Charismatic leaders or monarchs also asserted themselves in some cases.

The parliamentary form in India, however, is persisting, notwithstanding its imperialist mould. There are two important reasons for this. First, it has successfully co-opted the emerging elite so far. Second, even as physical limits of co-option have been reached, there is continuous change in the overt form of interest groups in the power structure. Each group gets busy in protecting or extending its share without challenging the frame. The people are taken in by slogans, unaware about the implications of the imperialist mould of their representative institutions.

A lot of confusion has been created in relation to nationality issue itself. In many countries, it has detracted the people from other basic issues. Such situations, therefore, have been consciously created by neo-imperialist capitalist forces to facilitate consolidation of their gains for making further inroads in these battered systems.

The most distinguishing feature of global political economy at the moment is that people everywhere are pitched against a centralized system, which has assumed an identity independent of the people. The difference in the relative order of 'power' which the two sides wield is very large. The growing imbalance and the insignificance of the people is a logical corollary of this difference. It is only on rare occasions that forces may get engendered on people's side sufficiently strong to overwhelm the system.

The Present System

The existing system aspiring for global hegemony is a product of the capitalistic logic under an imperialistic umbrella. Some of the salient features can be summarized as under:

1. *Alienation of the worker from means of production*: The process of alienation of worker from the means of production struck those depending upon natural resources for their living. These resources were grabbed physically by feudal lords in the first instance. The *de jure* claim over the same was perfected later by the State. The elimination of cultivator-farmer, stripping him of all residual claims, which he was able to protect in the face of earlier onslaughts, has been actively pursued by the capitalist system from its very inception. This take over of natural resources has been attempted in our country so far.
2. *Disappearance of craftsmen in the face of competition*: Rural industrial workers, artisans and craftsmen are also

disappearing from our country in the face of relentless competition from machine-made goods with the opening up of even remote regions and penetration of market in all spheres of man's life. Moreover, there is a qualitative change even in the conventional industrial system in the wake of quick succession of technological revolutions and deepening of capital in all production systems. The labourer has not only been alienated from the means of production, but is being rendered virtually redundant from many a field. Robots of all descriptions are replacing him, making the command of capital on the production system total and undisputed.

If we accept that the system is for welfare of the people, what needs to be probed is transformation of everything in public interest. The new system is incapable of accommodating all the people of the developing countries. Indian economy which has been largely following the West, notwithstanding the valiant efforts to guide its course through planning, has already entered the phase of 'jobless growth'. With production and consumption of physical goods and services as the measure of development, benefits are going to capitalist countries with adverse effects to developing states. This system has become non-sustainable. The world economy and national economy are moving in a direction in which a very small section of population will be required to work the economic system. In fact, the socially useful part of population will comprise only a small fraction thereof. What will be rest of the humanity be engaged in?

There must be a shift in the structure of the system itself. The system is moving towards total centralization of power. All the people on the globe will have nothing which they could claim as their own except perhaps their own labour. And even that labour would be redundant. There can be no real claims of the people in such a system unless it can be said that the system is a creation of the people's will and is at their command.

Search for the Missing Key

Production, profit and productivity are necessary concomitant of the present-day development which has resulted in concentration of economic and political power. It has also created inequality in society. They have been tolerated in the interest of faster growth. But, the greatest damage which has been done in the process is non-utilization, non-development or even non-recognition of the people's potential. Human development has been neglected. Human values have eroded, community is disorganized and even family has collapsed.

There have been social movements against working of the system. The continuance of the centralized power structure of the colonial era even after independence also evoked considerable criticism among political activists. It was echoed even in the Constituent Assembly which culminated in the enshrining of village panchayats as institutions of self-governance in the Indian Constitution. The people's reaction against the centralized power and even their anger and wrath against the same, as in tribal areas, was diverted into demand for regional, ethnic and linguistic formations. The biggest sin which has been committed in post-independence India, is the trivialization of the most fundamental issue of village self-governance under the cover of Panchayati Raj.

Movements of landless labour against social inequity, untouchability, access to natural resources including land, water and forest which comprise the main source of subsistence for the bulk of people in rural areas have been there. Other struggles have been for share in development in the form of reservation in services and other opportunities. All these movements related to malfunctioning of the system.

Major new struggles concern displacement directly related to development. The most notable movements in this category are against projects such as Sardar Sarovar, Tehri and a host of other river valley projects, mining projects such as Gandhamardan, defence establishments such as Balliapal and field firing range of Netarhat, industrial establishment such as Gopalpur, fisheries resources such as in the Chilka lake and Kerla fisherfolks. Most of these movements are largely confined to the problem of displacement. They do not question the authority of the state regarding command and use of resources but there was no clear stand about the alternatives. The oustees were to claim cash compensation and resettlement. Their source of livelihood was snatched and they were rendered homeless, landless and jobless.

The movement of village self-governance in the tribal areas has the potential of graduating into a pan-Indian people's movement which may force the ruling elite for a basic structural transformation. It gives expression to people's aspirations, their desire to understand, plan, execute and evaluate. Moreover, the resources on which people subsist for their living cannot be treated as property; that the people have an inherent natural right over the same as a means of livelihood which is superior to state's claim.

The idea of inalienable right of the people to use resources for their livelihood, the questioning of displacement for development which essentially means alternative use of resources, the right of self-governance lose much of their significance without command over the habitat. Concentration of wealth and economic power goes against the constitutional provision of Article 39 which enjoins the state the responsibility to ensure that the community resources are so used as to subserve the common good. Moreover, it is now asserted that that the command or ownership of the community are non-negotiable. A person can best assume the role of a manager but the resource vests in the community. With community and family as basic units, new process of development may start which is imbued with the ideals enshrined in the Constitution of India and is dedicated to the enrichment of the cultural life of the people and realization of the full potential of every person unrelated to money and market.

References

Edwards, Michael and Alan Fowler (eds.), *The Earthscan Reader on NGO Management*, Earth Scan, London, 2002.

Kapoor, A.K, *Rural Development Through NGOs*, Rawat Publications, Jaipur and New Delhi.

Lawani, B.T., *NGOs in Development*, Rawat Publications, Jaipur.

Sharma, B.D., *The People and The Systems*, Sahyog Pustak Kutir, New Delhi.

3

Need for Community Water Management

It is painful to note that about 20 per cent of the world community, 1.2 billion people, are without access to safe drinking water. Most of these people live in developing countries. The recent World Summit on Sustainable Development at Johannesburg has fixed the millennium development goals to reduce the uncovered population with drinking water by 50 per cent by the year 2015.

Since independence, India became a welfare state. After exploitation of natural resources by colonial rulers who never cared for their development, the Indian nation interested in development of Indian economy, took upon itself the responsibility of fully harnessing the available natural resources in the best interest of the community. We were importing even food grains from Australia and other countries to feed our population. Meeting shortage of food grains was the first priority. Hence, the prime sector for development was agriculture. All the cultivable land was to be allotted to the landless poor. Improved seed and chemical fertilizer inputs were popularized. Both the zamindari and jagirdari systems were abolished. Surplus land was allotted to the landless who subsequently became tenants. Irrigation projects were started to provide water through canals. Dams like Bhakra Nangal and Hirakud were constructed to save people from havoc caused by river water and divert it for irrigation of barren lands and thereby increase food production for the teeming millions in India.

Planned Development for Harnessing Water Resources

Looking from historical perspective, the first phase was that of civil engineers when construction of big irrigation dams was undertaken for storage of river water and diverting it for irrigation of farmer's fields. The second phase was developing experience of irrigation department in maintaining the canals, regulating the water supply, collecting the water rates and professional orientation of the irrigation department. Agricultural department became very active through extension services in the form of various improved agricultural practices, supply of hybrid seeds, propagating chemical fertilizers, supply of subsidized pesticides for plant protection in case of spread of diseases. All such efforts brought results. Green revolution was ushered into India. Food production multiplied many times to an extent that we have become self-sufficient in food grains in spite of constant increase in our population to an extent of 2.8 per cent every year. Now, the third phase came. People wanted assured water. There were lapses on behalf of the government machinery. Sometimes, breaches in canals were reported. Influential farmers manipulated the water distribution system.

The increase in irrigation potential in India has been a phenomenal four-fold since 1951. Irrigation water proved to be one of the most important inputs for ushering in green revolution. During this period, almost an exclusive emphasis was placed on construction of irrigation infrastructure. India today has the largest area under irrigation in the world. However, because of over-involvement with construction activities only, the aspects relating to management of irrigation were lost sight of, resulting in several problems such as unreliable and inequitable supply of water to farmers, poor maintenance of systems, poor recovery of water rates, increasing conflicts between irrigators, water logging of command areas, etc.

The main challenge is to get assured and timely water from its source of acquisition to the farmer's fields. As the land is not fully occupied during the first few years, neither land nor water presents a binding constraint. We saw in case of Rajasthan canal where lands were allotted to refugees and ex-service people but looking to initial problem of huge expenditure and labour involved in turning the barren soils into productive lands, they sold out land to others. Moreover, water requirement increases only after land levelling. The farmers were also new to the scheme and got acquainted over a period of time. Subsequently in the second stage, the land gets levelled and farmers are also settled and the knowledge of farmers regarding crops and need of water increases. The role of agronomist becomes more important and maximum return from land as a resource is expected by farmers. In the third stage, the system matures. Land becomes fully developed. Population is much denser. Water becomes a critical constraint, even more than land. Even when there is shortage of land, intensive agriculture can be resorted to. But it also needs water. Technological development also needs scientific use of water resources. Human factor becomes central in water management.

Former President of India, Dr. K.R. Narayanan, while inaugurating a conference organized by the Centre for Science and Environment on 'Potential of Water Harvesting' at New Delhi, on 3 October 1998 that warned the nation "this (water) universal asset is being fast depleted. Leading experts on water resources have been warning that the world is heading towards a 'water shock' which may dwarf the oil crisis. Some 80 countries and 40 per cent of the world's population is already experiencing 'water stress'. Environmental degradation and population explosion are making the problem even more acute, with pollution poisoning the water that is available".

Need for the Community Involvement

Former President of India, Dr. K.R. Narayanan stressed upon people's participation emphasizing that "India today needs a people's movement to meet its water needs and to protect its water sources.... We must get every community involved both in the provision of water and in the protection of water sources ....Civil society has to play a critical role in encouraging equity and sustainability in the use of water...." Increase in human and bovine population of the country has resulted not only in reduction of per capita availability of net area cultivated, but also in substantial reduction in availability of common properties for grazing for the cattle and shortage of fuel wood for domestic purposes. There have also been increasing number of cases of grabbing of common lands by influential people of the villages. In earlier years after independence, the pressure on lands was not so much because there was enough land available for people as well as cattle, nobody thought of reclaiming waste lands or conserving flowing waters, but after increased demand for agriculture and diminishing water levels, need for management of natural resources has become imminent. The present status of management of forests, land and water is a big question mark, since environment is degrading fast in spite of the best efforts of the government and biomass is almost disappearing not only from the pastures but also from reserved forests, what to talk of unreserved forests. Hence, it is already high time that the community, in the common interest, should come forward to protect common property resources to save it from the shackles of unscrupulous hands. Community should come forward boldly for management of natural resources to get maximum and purposeful returns from land, water and forest.

Development plans and changing living pattern during the last few decades in India have caused negative impact on our environment. As a result of it – disturbance has been caused in seasons, rains have been affected, forests have degenerated, catchment area of watershed areas has been dislocated. In spite of squandering crores of rupees on water harvesting structures and water storage dams, expected results are not visible. Problem villages have increased even for drinking water. Number of flood affected villages have also multiplied. Community organizations for managing water resources have become weak and even government efforts have not been able to achieve complete success.

Water which is a community resource, is being treated as a state monopoly and is given to people only as a 'gift'. It is being sold as a commodity. Both World Bank and International Monetary Fund have been advancing huge cheap loans for development to India, hence under international pressure of free world economy and globalization, Indian government may sell out water resources to private foreign companies. Argentina is a living example of privatization of water. Water supply was handed over to a French company 'Vivendi' as a result of which price of water per unit increased from 24 peso to 59 peso. The company invested money also from government loan. People were enraged, went on strike and subsequently the company had to leave. Example of Kocha Bamba City of Bolivia is there, where water was privatized and private companies were made owners of water in place of community. During the World Trade Conference held at Doha, ministerial level discussions were held regarding privatization of water to remove the hindrances in framing the policy of privatization. Recently framed water policy in India is based on discussions held in Doha conference. Hence, there is a necessity to restore water resource to the community to whom it really belongs.

As against such need of the community, management of natural resources was either absent or highly centralized and with hierarchical bureaucracy. The farming community is also dissatisfied with the service rendered by irrigation and water supply departments. Distribution of water has become unpredictable, unreliable and inequitable. The system is also suffering from low returns on capital invested by the government and is unable to meet huge salary of staff and other maintenance expenditure required for smooth running of such projects. Poor management has led to less than expected productivity. Moreover, scarce water is not utilized efficiently because there is neither any incentive nor motivation in the existing system.

In such a historical process, the role of government should evolve from that of being a system's manager to that of being a service provider. Farmers should move from water recipients to water users and then as water co-managers along with irrigation department. But this is not an easy process for agencies to accommodate beneficiaries and make space for so-called reserved domain of administration. There can be many ups and downs in performance and examples of success and failures may be there. But participation is essential in view of prevailing conditions, specially when it is not possible for the state to maintain the irrigation as well as drinking water infrastructure due to financial constraints. This is true of not only India but other countries in the world also. It is now felt that one of the most important reason for these problems is lack of stakeholders' participation in water management. It is now believed that no worthwhile management of irrigation as well as drinking water is possible without participation of beneficiaries of water.

The Government of India organized National Conferences on Participatory Irrigation Management in 1995, 1997 and 1999 at New Delhi and Hyderabad. It was commonly accepted that the message of participatory management needs to be taken to all sections of the society, since improved systems of water delivery management is the only panacea of existing problems. Improved and efficient water management is becoming more and more vital as one moves in the 21st century with growing population and diverse users of water, placing more and more pressure on the available water resources. The scope for construction of new dams has reduced because most of such sites have already been tapped and there is increasing resistance on environmental grounds and displacement of inhabitants of submerged areas. If the available water is not used most efficiently and wastage eliminated, as far as possible, a large population in India may face water stress. Adoption of methods for efficient and optimal use of water brooks no delay.

Participatory Management of Water Resources

We cannot think of sustainability of any community without proper use of land, water and other natural resources. Even if the natural resources are abundant, proper distribution of land and water resources alone can deliver the goods in a welfare state like India. In spite of planned development in India and construction of big irrigation dams, we are facing problems of waterlogging and salinity in canal areas due to excessive irrigation. In river areas the excessive water during rainy season causes heavy dislocation and land losses during floods. There are areas which are dry for want of water. Even in canal areas, farmers having fields at the tail end of canals crying for scarcity of water for irrigation. Community management of water resources can be a means for proper management and equitable distribution of rain and irrigation water.

Participatory management of water resources may not be panacea for all water management issues, but yet it can go a long way in ensuring efficient running of canals, optimum on-field water application and proper drainage of excess water from irrigation systems and farmers' fields. Such participatory management can work only if all the stakeholders – farmers, irrigation agency employees including engineers, government, etc., feel that participatory management will further their individual and group or community interests, both singly and jointly. Farmers should feel an urge to come together in water user associations and to take over water management functions. Government employees should realize the need to change the ways. Training and orientation of both farmers as well as irrigation or other water agencies is needed for preparing all the stakeholders for success of participatory management.

The role of government institutions in the management of water resources is changing partly due to two trends:

1. Most governments around the world are confronted with the reality of decline in fiscal capabilities. They do not have adequate financial and personnel resources to continue to operate water management systems as directly as in the past.
2. With increase in literacy levels and general consciousness among cultivators and community, people have been capable enough to take care of mutual interest and manage community affairs to the best of their capability. At the most, some orientation will build their capacity to manage things well.

Though, farmers cannot design main reservoirs or main canals, nor should they try. But there can be consultation with representatives even on technical matters. Sprinkler irrigation might be difficult to plan, but drip irrigation systems might be improved through farmer participation. When it comes to laying out or rehabilitating channels, farmer inputs can be particularly useful.

Governments of Mexico, Turkey, Nepal, Philippines and Sri Lanka are also trying experience of distribution of such responsibilities with the user beneficiaries. Efforts should be made to push this process along, though it should not be done too fast. In general, state governments should withdraw from doing things that farmers can handle,

1. to reduce the costs of organization and maintenance but also

2. to fine-tune operation and maintenance (O&M), since users have more detailed knowledge of local conditions and have more stake and motivation to utilize available resources more efficiently.

Example of running Pani Panchayats in Maharashtra has exemplified how farmers made optimum utilization of irrigation waters and assured irrigation of at least two acres to each farmer in drought conditions.

This process should not be seen as irrigation or PHED department losing control over water and as giving up their responsibilities. Rather, control is exercised more indirectly but probably more effectively because government will now become a 'wholesaler' of water rather than a 'retailer'. A more participatory system of management should be able to save money and provide better service, if provision is made for accountable systems of organization.

Objectives of Community Water Management

- Right of water to the community and responsibility of the community to conserve water and equitably distribute among members.
- Create awareness regarding associating people with rivers rather than joining of inter-state rivers.
- Recharging groundwater through sharing past experiences of benefits of water conservation projects executed by the community.
- Get such water policy prepared at the government level in which community participation is ensured and water is treated as a joint property with the community.
- Right for use of water for those who conserve water.
- Create awareness among people regarding water conservation and create community forum for water management.

References

Centre for Science and Environment, New Delhi, Proceedings of the Conference on Potential of Water Harvesting, 3-5 October, 1998.

Edwards, Michael and Alan Fowler (eds.), *The Earthscan Reader on NGO Management*, Earthscan, London, 2002.

Joshi, L.K. and Rakesh Hooja (eds.), *Participatory Irrigation Management*, Rawat Publications, Jaipur and New Delhi, 2000.

Mishra, G.P. and Bajpai, B.K. (eds.), *Community Participation in Natural Resource Management*, Rawat Publications, Jaipur and New Delhi, 2001.

Singh, Rajendra, *National Water Awareness Journey*, Tarun Bharat Sangh, 2003.

4

Community Participation in Water Resource Management: Past Experiences

Presently, more than 70 per cent population is directly dependent on agriculture, animal husbandry and related activities. Therefore, it is very important that natural resources like land, water, forests, crops, animals and human beings remain in focus of development. The natural resources especially land, water and forests are under acute pressure and more so in drought years. Erratic rains have adversely affected food production and food security. This results into over exploitation of available limited resources.

Conflicts over natural resources have intensified during recent years in many parts of the Third World. Development measures have not kept pace with population growth. Competing demands by different claimants on same resources result in conflicts. The case of state governments of Tamil Nadu and Karnataka is before us, who recently approached the Supreme court on the issue of distribution of Cauvery waters for irrigation. Numerous such conflicts over river waters continue to pose a threat to peace and stability in several parts of the Third World.

We see a major role in organizing people in rural areas for management of natural resources in a sustainable manner. Natural resources are best conserved when people dependent on them for their survival are keenly involved in their management and conservation. Recent years have therefore witnessed an increasing accent on community based natural resource management at national as well as international levels. Community-based natural resource management is characterized by:

1. Increased partnership with the community through community based organizations and Panchayat Raj Institutions (PRIs).
2. Availability of information, knowledge and technology.
3. Research and extension of locally useful techniques.
4. Suitable government policies and programmes.
5. Availability of timely inputs and services.

All-round and large-scale development of communities requires a combination of efforts and approaches which cannot be solely provided by one agency or system. To ensure that the benefits of development reach the poor, in particular, and the people in general, it is necessary that different agencies working for development, pool their strengths and become partners.

India's forest policy of 1988 represents a major shift in the conservation and management strategy of forests in so far as it advocates a community participation approach, for the first time since scientific forestry began in 1864. Introduction of Joint Forest Management (JFM) system in 17 out of 25 states of India is a major shift from the state regulation towards community participation in forest management. It seeks to strengthen the relationship of people living in and around the forests on a sustainable and exploitative basis. JFM conveys economic benefits of the forests to the local people as a matter of right and not as a concession. The policy provides that the requirement of fuel wood, fodder, minor forest produce and small timber of the rural and tribal population should be the first charge on the forests which really belong to the community. The forest department is to provide necessary funds for plantation and employment generating activities.

Since the recommendations of Hanumant Rao Committee in 1994, all watershed development programmes were placed in the hands of the community through people's watershed development committees to plan and execute the projects. Wasteland development has also been ordered to be executed through village development committees.

Panchayats (Extension to Scheduled Areas) Act, 1996 was enacted placing all the natural resources of minor forest produce, minor water bodies, fisheries, mines, lands at the disposal of the Gram Sabha which means the community. Madhya Pradesh also enacted Panchayat Raj and Gram Swaraj Act, 2001 placing land, water and forest resources at the disposal of Gram Sabha as per Section 129 of the Act. The states of Gujarat, Maharashtra, Himachal Pradesh, Rajasthan and Orissa having tribal areas therein are following the same line of vesting natural resources at the disposal of the community for management in tribal areas.

Rajiv Gandhi Foundation Drinking Water Mission along with donor agencies gave priority to community-based drinking water supply schemes. Sector Reform Project was initiated in 55 districts of India including four districts of Alwar, Sikar, Rajsamand and Jaipur (Rajasthan) in the first instance some four years ago. Since 26 January 2003, it has been started in all the districts under the new nomenclature of *Swajaldhara*. The scheme envisages 10 per cent contribution by the community and complete planning, execution and management of the water supply scheme by the rural community.

Thus, community management is becoming increasingly pertinent in the management of common property resources. Though ownership and management of these resources rested with the state for a long time, the government's failure to preserve common property resources together with their excessive exploitation for development has led to serious degradation of the environment with the attendant ecological repercussions. Under people's participation as an alternative, the beneficiaries are made responsive to the cost of preservation. Such a system makes development with preservation possible.

In such background, conservation, management and development of natural resources on a scientific basis is essential to ensure a sustainable development process of the country. Management of natural resources must meet the basic requirements of people on an equitable basis without causing environmental damage.

Natural resources cannot be managed and preserved properly without involving the rural communities which derive their sustenance from the natural resources. Land, water and forest are really the source of livelihood of people in rural areas. They cannot be utilized for commercial purposes by the state. Community has the right to use it for their subsistence. The aim of the land use policy is to provide supportive technological and institutional structures to enable these rural communities to manage the resources in an optimum manner.

Community natural resource management system has existed in the historical past. New people-based initiatives have also emerged widely in recent years. The Van Panchayats of Kumaon, Pani Panchayats of Maharashtra, Sukho Majri experiment in Haryana and Ralegaon Sidhi of Maharashtra, Gopalpura in Alwar (Rajasthan), Arabari in West Bengal and JFM committees of Orissa, Chipko in Himachal Pradesh, Vankar cooperatives of Gujarat are some of the well-known examples of participatory efforts of the people. In above cases, people put an end to free grazing, developed wastelands through water and soil conservation and revitalized agriculture, animal husbandry, horticulture, etc., and shared common benefits of tree growing.

Ralegaon Sidhi Project in Maharashtra

Ralegaon Sidhi is perhaps India's first model of watershed development initiated in 1975 by Padma Shree Anna Hazare and fostered by local community. Ralegaon Sidhi was a drought-prone village with a small population of 2,100 persons. Conservation of rain water was given the highest priority and the community constructed a series of 31 check dams and *nala bunds*. Not only water was stored but it tremendously raised the water level. Community wells were dug out of which water was supplied at moderate rates; two crops were raised. Fruits and vegetables could also be grown which are now exported to Dubai. No one migrates out of the village in search of employment. The villagers have completely stopped grazing of cattle on common lands and shifted to stall-feeding. Fodder supply has increased as its result. Tree felling is completely stopped and about 2 lakh new trees have been planted on hill slopes. Fuel, fodder and fruits are available, while soil erosion is checked. Main reason for positive impact on crops, milk yield, fodder, employment and income is whole-hearted community participation in the form of *shramdaan* and cash in the project.

Sukho Majri Experiment in Haryana

The people living in and around the catchment of Sukhna lake of the city of Chandigarh were facing severe environmental hazards. People residing in the catchment area of the lake suffered from low agricultural production and lack of irrigation facility. There was free grazing. Fuelwood cutting and poor maintenance of forest resulted in soil erosion also. Cattle and goats were the main source of livelihood. People were poor and in great tension.

Around 1981, an institution named Hill Resources Management Society was formed consisting of one member from each household. The community constructed two small dams to collect rain water which was used for irrigating the area. Later, a big dam was also constructed. The crop yield increased due to irrigation facility. Availability of grass and fodder was more. Fuel wood also increased. Milk yield of the cattle also increased thereby. Water User Associations (WUAs) emerged in 1981 and ensured equal distribution of water. Persons with no land could sell their water to others who needed it. Grass cutting contract was also given to village society in 1983 by the forest department. Community participation worked wonders in the economy of Sukho Majri which is a model in micro watershed development project in the country.

Chipko Movement in Himachal Pradesh

Chipko movement is a rare experiment made by women of Gopeshwar. A woman member from each household have a forum, Mahila Mangal Dal under Dasholi Gram Swarajya Mandal. Women of the village get together, discuss their problem, seek their solutions and assert their priorities. Village groups have taken control of community lands surrounding their villages. They protect these lands, plant trees on them and ensure fair distribution of grass and fodder among them. It is available in larger quantity. Against tree cutting, women stuck to the trunks of the trees at the point of death. Hence, it is known as 'Chipko'. After afforestation, activities of provision of drinking water, schools and health facility are also executed as a part of the programme activity.

Vankar Cooperatives in Gujarat

In Bhal area of Gujarat, co-operatives of villages have been executing afforestation programmes in the highly saline lands under the guidance of St. Xavier's Behavioural Centre of Ahmedabad. The co-operatives consist of members of all households of the scheduled caste community of Vankars residing in these villages. Afforestation has been done on community lands of Vankars. Land was lying idle since it was allotted to SCs by the government. Due to salinity, no crop was grown. *Prosopis juliflora* was planted. Poor Vankars convert wood into charcoal, earn money and live well with community effort.

Gram Dan Experiment of Seed in Udaipur (Rajasthan)

Rajasthan Gram Dan Act, 1971 entrusts all lands to Gram Sabha who elect a President and revenue administration is also managed by the Gram Sabha. Decisions are taken by common consensus. Land is divided into three categories:

1. Open common area where grazing is permitted but tree felling is prohibited by order of the Gram Sabha.
2. Protected common area where all grazing and tree felling is prohibited by order of the Gram Sabha.
3. Private agricultural fields where tree felling needs prior permission from Gram Sabha.

The first category of land remains lush green and full of grass which villagers cut only once a year. Grass is equitably distributed among the households. The area is hilly. Fine is imposed by Gram Sabha for violation of above rules. Similar practice is also in vogue in watershed development projects executed in most of the villages of Udaipur district. All this has become possible because of the community effort.

Peepalwas Watershed Project in Udaipur, Rajasthan

It was a small area of 86.29 hectares only of which 80 per cent area was rain fed with deep water strata and hard rocks. Only 20 per cent was irrigated. Climate is semi-arid and the area suffered from poor crop husbandry.

Watershed Resource Society was formed. It prepared plans with expert technical guidance. Soil and water conservation was ensured by seeding of grass, terracing, loose stone check dams, afforestation after stone fencing, water harvesting and spillways in fields. Change in land use pattern resulted in soil and water conservation, crop intensity and productivity increased, per capita income increased by 68.33 per cent (Rs. 598 to Rs. 1,739 per family). Benefit Cost ratio was 1.76:1.

Best National Productivity Council Award Winning Watersheds of Rajasthan

Watershed and wasteland development projects are executed by all the states and are evaluated at the national level by a high-powered committee. During following years, watersheds of Rajasthan were adjudged as the best in India and they were awarded National Productivity Council best award at the national level.

Year	*Name of watershed*	*Award*
1992-93	Losing (Udaipur)	Best watershed of the country for the year
1994-96	Kotri (Bhilwara)	Best Rajiv Gandhi Wasteland Development Project of the country for the year
1995-96	Kamli (Rajsamand)	Best watershed of the country for the year
1996-97	Balesaria (Bhilwara)	Best watershed of the country for the year
1998-99	Dumara (Ajmer)	Best watershed of the country for the year

Main Features of Community Management of Watersheds

- General awareness camps.
- Visit to successful watershed areas to arouse interest about utility of watershed development project.
- Entry point activities to associate people with the project.
- Formation of homogenous self-help groups of water users, animal breeders, shepherds, women, nursery groups and such other beneficiaries having common interest in the project.
- Group meetings to identify group needs and prepare plan accordingly as per felt needs of the villagers.
- Participatory rural appraisal of local resources.
- Formation of Watershed Development Committee from amongst the beneficiaries.

- Preparing need-based plan.
- Entrusting responsibility for execution of the programmes among different groups by the Watershed Development team (WDT).
- Actual execution in the field.
- Monitoring by members of the committee and collecting contribution from members.
- Conserving 10 per cent development fund for maintenance of assets after completion of the project.

The following main features regarding community participation and management was observed in the best adjudged national watersheds:

1. Grasslands were developed on a large scale by seeding of grass on common lands.
2. Cutting of dry grass was regulated from watershed areas.
3. No one is allowed to graze cattle in the watershed areas.
4. Community imposes and recovers penalty for violation of grazing regulations.
5. *Ber* budding and plantation of trees was found very successful on hills and pastures.
6. Members of the society often meet to discuss issues relating to management of common property resources and overall development of the village.
7. Excess water from cultivated fields was diverted through channels.
8. Society is running smoothly with active people's participation to manage common property resources.

People-centred NGO Initiative in Sustainable Rural Development: The Case of Rangabelia Project in West Bengal

The Rangabelia project has been working in 256 villages of seven blocks covering a population of 2.10 lakhs, 41,200 families in Sundarbans islands of West Bengal. It is an NGO effort which has become a sort of a model participatory approach to sustainable development in a typical agro-climatic region such as Sundarbans. In the official approach, economic gains are not sustained mainly because it is target-oriented and area-specific; bureaucracy believes in top down approach which may suffer from leakages and inefficiencies. There is virtually no participation by the target group at any level of the programmes, whereas in Rangabelia project, people were at the centre of activity – group members worked intensively at the lowest level, 'para' (ward or mohalla) at the middle level and project authority at the top. There was full involvement of beneficiaries at every stage and every level.

Sundarban's South 24 Parganas region had 54 islands, saline sub-soil water, 3 million people, almost no electricity, mono cropped, 70 per cent poor population, abject poverty due to floods and cyclones, insufficient income generating capacity, 70 per cent families indebted to money lenders and lands mortgaged, people suffering from water borne diseases, high infant mortality (130 per 1,000) and high death rate (40 per 1,000) till 1975 when the project started. Tushar Kanjilal joined as head master of a high school in 1968 and soon became friendly with the local people. He became a guide to poor people in organizing them. In 1975, Tagore Society for Rural Development launched a project from Rangabelia. Initial seed capital was provided by a German funding organization and Government of India and the State Government also supported. NGO workers were sincere and devoted. There are 162 workers attached with the project.

Phase I (1975-78)

Detailed economic survey was done by dedicated workers led by head master Kanjilal. Mobilization of landless poor peasants and awareness building among women was on priority. People dug more ponds and canals for storing rain water and cultivation of winter paddy crops on mortgaged lands in four villages spread over seven islands of Rangabelia. An environment of confidence was created. People took collective initiative to move into wider areas of action. Health and hygiene issues, safe drinking water, kitchen garden and poultry were undertaken during this phase. Mahila Samiti (Women's Organization) started income generating programmes. Local talents were encouraged. Struggle against exploiters started.

Phase II (1978-1989)

Resource base in terms of land, water, animals, birds, trees, tools and implements, finance (own and borrowed), human asset was defined. The object was to utilize and augment resource base. Intensive efforts were made at economic upliftment involving human engineering at the individual, family and group levels. Groups of 10-15 members were formed. One became group secretary to record proceedings of the group meetings to be held every week. Family wise individual resources were listed in terms of income, expenditure, indebtedness, health data etc. Twice a year, on the eve of monsoon crop and winter crop, crop planning was done. Additional physical and financial resources to be borrowed from the project were listed and provided. Various aspects of management of each type of family level repayment schedule and estimated additional income etc. were calculated. Each family would maintain daily income and expenditure. Weekly meetings of every group were held to monitor family level plans under the guidance of NGO workers. Proceedings of group meetings were recorded. 'Para' meetings were held every fortnight to discuss and sort out common issues and forward to project office. By 1988, more than 1,000 groups were working in 57 villages along with few exclusive women groups for thrift, saving and health issues of child and mother. Phase II depended on loan-cum-subsidy and 3-tier bottom-up participatory organization worked successfully. Group at the bottom, 'para' at the middle and project authority at the top.

Phase III (since 1989)

During 1988 severe cyclone and floods devastated the efforts undertaken so far. There was massive destruction of life and property, homes and animals. Larger issues of ecological and environmental degradation came up. Regular awareness camps were held in different islands and villages. Massive meetings of people were organized in the Sunderbans region. Conventions of political groups, bureaucrats, ministers, professional experts and people were arranged. 'Greening programme' of planting economically useful trees was undertaken. Two-storey school buildings were constructed to serve as 'Flood Protection Centres'. Scientific designing of thatched homes to withstand high speed wind was also done. Scientific agriculture and regular soil testing by farmers was practised.

People-centred participatory development took place with active involvement of people. Popular participation of beneficiaries remained a guiding principle throughout, in Rangabelia project. Unique 'indigenization' of the development process from the very beginning has been the greatest strength of Rangabelia project. Beneficiary participation and involvement at almost all stages and all levels have been achieved and institutionalized through regular group meetings – 'para' meetings, workers' meetings and camps, awareness camps, training camps, mass meetings twice a year, interaction of project workers with the people and above all, unique electrifying and humorous personality of Tushar Kanjilal.

There were internal conflicts, different views and personal interests, malice, misunderstandings but all this was resolved and absorbed by the group through reasoned deliberations. Tushar Kanjilal has always avoided issuing mandates and sorting out issues democratically and in good humour.

During the project period 1976 to 1994 (period of study under report), birth rate fell from 40 to 26 per 1,000, death rate from 20 to 9, child mortality from 130 to 32 per 1,000, and incidence of water borne diseases reduced by 80 per cent.

Consumption of fertilizers rose from 3.15 kg to 6.30 kg per family. Tractors and power tillers increased from 250 to 2,500 and mechanized farming from 175 to 2,000 acres.

Major reason for all such achievements was human engineering and growth of local leadership among men and women. Invaluable leadership of Tushar Kanjilal, devoted team of workers and urge among local people to improve were dominant factors for success. Any model of sustainable development which focuses on the people as their primary concern, should not stop at providing them with livelihood alone. Unless people's awareness, attitudes and perceptions towards the ecology and environment are changed, sustainable development will be a distant dream.

Arabari Joint Forest Management Committee of West Bengal

Success of the pilot experiment on Arabari range of Midnapore district of West Bengal provided a basis for subsequent official JFM. Local villagers were motivated to form Forest Protection Committee to protect public *sal coppice* forests in return for first preference in forestry department, free usufruct rights to most minor forest products and 25 per cent share in net cash benefits from sales of short rotation sal poles when these were ready for harvesting. Initial success led to its expansion to neighbouring areas. Grazing was not done in the forest area. It provided viable livelihood alternatives needed to enable the villagers to stop unsuitable forest exploitation and care for forest protection on community basis.

Environment Development through People's Participation, Purulia, West Bengal

Ramakrishna Mission Lokashiksha Parishad, Narendrapur, West Bengal has done a yeoman's service by organizing voluntary 'youth clubs' in all the villages to organize people, make them aware about wasteland development, raising crops, preparing farmer nurseries, forest plantation, organizing Forest

Protection Committees, ensuring rights for non-timber products and thereby empowering community. Swami Vivekanand gave a slogan:

> The only service to be done for our lower classes is to give them education, to develop their lost identity.... They are to be given ideas; their eyes are to be opened to what is going on in the world around them; and then they will work out their own salvation. Every nation, every man, and every woman must work out their own salvation. Give them ideas – that is the only help they require....

The Mission started the work of environmental development in early 1980s. Substantial progress was made in this endeavour when the National Wasteland Development and Integrated Watershed Development Programmes were undertaken on a massive scale in the district of Purulia (West Bengal) which underwent massive degradation in terms of reduction of forest area and subsequently erosion of soil. In 60 villages covering 11 blocks of Purulia, 2,592 families were involved. About 1,000 hectares of privately owned wastelands have been greened by planting about 29 lakh plants with different models of afforestation since 1987. Farm forestry with Akasmani and eucalyptus was initially chosen by most people in a monoculture system. With the introduction of an agro-forestry system with Arjuna as forest plant and pigeon pea, black gram and niger, etc., as agricultural crops, people's choice gradually diversified. The later model created a good amount of sensation among people because of its efficiency in generation of employment, income, production of biomass for fuel and cocoon for agro-based cottage industry generating employment for women, besides, greening the lands and protecting soil from erosion. A range of plant species were planted including Akasmani, Babul, Siris, Neem, Sishu, Subabool, Eucalyptus, Kusum, Sal Arnuna, Asana, etc. Soil conservation measures with contour bunding was an essential feature in several locations. On-farm testing of regeneration of Sal from seeds employing pitcher drip was a special event of success. Simarauba, a new oil-seed plant species was also introduced by the Parishad. About 90 per cent work was done in district Purulia and 10 per cent in other districts of south and north 24-Parganas and Murshidabad. A large number of youth groups have been given awareness and technical training in the different aspects of afforestation. Their active participation at all stages of work was a key factor of success. As the youth groups gradually gained experience and confidence, other activities towards the promotion of employment and income generation were introduced. Primary youth groups worked as decentralized task forces at different levels with clusters with a central committee. Specific measures were taken to create awareness with the following kinds of activities:

- Meeting at the individual youth club level. Youth of both groups participate at all levels.
- Meeting at the cluster level (a central office of a group of youth clubs).
- Youth encounters at the Parishad level.
- Camps at the district level.
- Annual conference, etc.

In training programmes, not only general orientation is given but skill development, related to various aspects of afforestation including advance soil work, nursery technique, planting techniques, etc., are also imparted. Post-plantation work, soil and water conservation work, etc., are also taught. People's participation through youth groups was key to success. The involvement of the people was in the process of motivation, village level appraisal, planning of activities, selection of species, implementation of work and protection of plantation. In many cases the women youth workers responded very positively while asserting local needs through participatory sessions.

Methodology of wasteland development and the entire task of environmental protection and promotion followed the following steps:

- Identification of wastelands
- Formulation of beneficiaries' groups
- Training and orientation
- Field level assistance and guidance of the forest department
- Supervision and monitoring

Activities included strip plantation, farm forestry, agro-forestry, employment generation, artificial generation of sal, introduction of new plant species, etc. Year-wise achievements can be summarized in the following table:

Year	*Number of seedlings planted*	*Number of beneficiaries*	*Area planted (hect.)*	*Number of arjun seedlings planted*
1987	2,51,056	412	88.10	65,000
1988	5,50,479	445	205.45	90,000
1989	5,60,010	480	201.40	1,26,900
1990	4,92,950	240	158.10	61,000
1991	5,19,858	382	190.35	2,35,000
1992	4,23,085	426	115.75	67,575
1993	2,43,766	207	57.20	49,340

Overall survival percentage of plants is above 75 per cent. This was possible because of community participation mainly through youth clubs at different levels and their empowerment and guidance of the NGO like Ramakrishna Mission. It was all possible with financial assistance from the Ford Foundation and National Wastelands Development Board and help and cooperation of the forest department of West Bengal.

Community Action for Forest Management in Orissa

Almost in all districts of the state of Orissa, a large forest area of common property is managed by communities. Forest is community's life supporting system hence community initiatives have been taken in response to severe forest degradation. Generally, the villagers start protecting patches, which are considerably degraded but have the root stock intact. Favourable conditions conducive to community protection of forests were as under:

1. Presence of strong village organization for such an organization.
2. Unity in the village.
3. Scarcity of forest produce.
4. Mismanagement of reserved forests and poor control of the forest department.
5. Effect of other villages in which forest patches were being protected.

Orissa has maximum tribal population in the state and traditional panchayats of tribals take unanimous decisions. This is also a favourable factor in the state because forests are in hilly areas and tribals also inhabit in hilly areas near the forest. Tribals were already managing temple lands and tanks, hence it was easier to give control of forest also to the community. Youth clubs also protect the forest where informal village committees are not active. Funds are generated through sale of forest materials to the villagers at a cheaper rate. Fines collected for violation of rules also form a source of income of the village. Protection of patches of forest is done either by employing a watchman or practice voluntary patrolling on rotation basis. Rules are formulated by the community itself for regulating the use of forest patches. The strong community-based forest management system developed in Orissa testify to the fact that communities can effectively manage local resources.

Managing Groundwater for Irrigation: Case Study of Samraspur Village of Orissa

Community Dug-Well Irrigation Scheme in village of Cuttack district since 1971 is again a good example of people's participation. Cooperation along with community endeavour could ensure sustainable development and equitable use of water resources. Around 90 farmers having an area of 246.43 acres made a cooperative investment on 26 dug-wells with the loan assistance of Rs. 5,000 per family and subsidy from Land Development Bank and balance from their own manual labour. They got 33 per cent subsidy from District Rural Development Agency (DRDA) and 25 per cent special state subsidy since 91 per cent beneficiaries were small and marginal farmers.

Resource base of water for irrigation of the lands of the cultivators was restructured. There were 26 wells fitted with electric pumpsets. Diseconomies associated with individual production units were scaled down because of cooperative venture in credit and marketing, etc. Besides successful maintenance and operation of irrigation water, group management system ensured effective as well as profitable use of water resource.

Success Factors

- Socio-economically homogeneous class factor
- Urge for upliftment was a powerful stimulus
- Behavioural attitudes of cooperation

Cost was shared on area basis. Dry land became wet. Crop intensity increased. Multiple cropping could be possible. On-farm employment was provided. Productivity and income increased by 238.7 per cent (Rs. 763.94 to Rs. 1,823.59 per acre). It was basically due to community participation and cooperation among beneficiaries.

Pani Panchayats of Maharashtra

During 1972-73 the state of Maharashtra suffered one of the worst droughts. Purandar taluk of Pune district was not an exception but suffered acute shortage of water as well as food. An NGO, Gram Gaurav Parishad (GGP) developed the concept of Pani Panchayats. The first Panchayat was formed for a patch of 16 hectares of almost degraded temple land situated on the hill slopes in Nayagaon village of Purandar taluk. Five following principles were decided:

1. Only group irrigation schemes would be taken up on community basis.
2. Each member will be entitled to get water for half acre of irrigation with an upper ceiling of two and a half acres for a household.
3. Water rights are not attached to the land. In case of sale of land, the new owner will not get water rights. It was done to prevent the sale of land by poor persons due to economic compulsions.
4. Cost of the scheme would be borne between beneficiaries in the ratio of 2:4:4 – among beneficiaries: GGP: subsidy from the state. Beneficiaries will execute and operate the scheme.
5. Sugarcane and banana crops are prohibited since they consume more water. It will benefit maximum number of members and maximum land.

There are said be about 60 Pani Panchayats in Maharashtra at present. Pani Panchayats have considerably raised the income and employment. Cropping pattern and crop intensity has changed favourably. Distribution of water is equitable. High water consuming crops are absent. Community needs brought the villagers together and the experiment is running successfully.

Forest Panchayats of Uttranchal

The Forest Panchayats were formed in the districts of Almora, Pithora Garh and Nainital of Kumaon division and Chamoli and Pauri Garhwal of Garhwal division during the British rule in India in 1931. A Forest Panchayat consists of 5 to 9 members elected by the local people. The members elect their own Sarpanch for a period of five years. The Sub-divisional Officer is Forest Panchayat Officer and is assisted by forest inspectors. Panchayat checks indiscriminate cutting of forest, tampering of fencing by villagers, earmark trees for felling, prevent encroachment on forest panchayat lands, fix and maintain boundary pillars. Panchayats can sell grass, fallen twigs for firewood, resin tapping, auction fodder and trees up to a value of Rs. 500. But they are panchayats of elected people. Community is not involved directly.

Rejuvenation of Ruparel River in Thanagazi, Alwar in Rajasthan

Rajendra Singh, Magsaysay Award winner, is now known throughout the country for 'National Water Awareness Campaign 2002-03' for enlisting community awareness regarding water policy framed by the Government of India regarding engaging foreign companies on contract basis for supply of water. His NGO Tarun Bharat Sangh (TBS) is a group of devoted workers for forest and water conservation incessantly working through the community in villages of Thanaghazi tehsil of Alwar district in Rajasthan since 1975. By now, it has 43 full-time voluntary workers and about 5,000 community volunteers. TBS works for making villagers self-dependent. Self-dependence in agriculture comes through water, use of cowdung and local seeds. Along with water conservation, the community has also developed their local conventions for regulation of use of water. People take their own decisions at the community level now.

Ruparel river was a perennial river during the good old days when there was dispute between the rulers Alwar and Bharatpur states regarding sharing of river waters. Dispute was referred to the British court where it remained pending for four years when it was decided in 1928. But, after independence, due to cutting of forest and cultivation in the runway of water of the hills and withdrawal of concessions to villagers by the forest department, soil erosion resulted, cultivation also became impossible thereafter, people had to migrate from the village after rains, only women remained behind in the villages which were almost deserted. Ruparel river dries up from December to July though its total catchment is 3,250 sq.km. Gujars live in hills and rear cattle whereas the Meena community is engaged in agriculture. Workers of TBS started organizing the women in the villages (since 1975) for forest and water conservation. There was an acute famine from 1980 to 1985. There was no water in the villages. *Johad* (tank) was excavated by women of the village Mala Tolawas. During the first year, water remained for three months, during the second year it remained for 6-7 months and during the third it lasted for the whole year. Workers of TBS were also engaged in *shramdaan* with the women of the village. It prompted the villagers of other villages also to organize community effort.

TBS conducted journeys on foot and organized community for *shramdaan* during village meetings. They resisted even the forest department and constructed check dams for water conservation in their villages and excavated tanks. Drinking water became available, water level in the wells rose high and migration stopped. People were happy. Though only four check dams were constructed by the villagers through local technical knowledge in 1987, in all 21 anecuts, 240 *johad / johadi* (big and small check dams), one dam, one fishery pond and contour-bunding at more than 91 places were constructed by 1995 by the community under local guidance of community volunteers. No qualified engineer was ever engaged. It was a magic effect that Ruparel river flows for the whole year now, no one migrates out in search of employment; water and crops are available to villagers for sustenance of their life. It is an exemplary case of community participation in the recent past.

All these success stories prove that community alone cannot achieve results unless some devoted social activists form a group of sincere workers who work incessantly in rural areas with missionary zeal. Motivation, guidance, training and support to community in the form of technical and financial assistance combined with involvement of local community and help and assistance by concerned government departments can create such examples.

References

Indian Journal of Regional Science, 1996, pp. 111-118.

Journal of Rural Development, 1995, pp. 385-408.

Journal of Rural Development, National Institute of Rural Development, Hyderabad,1995, pp. 107-116.

Mishra, G.P. and Bajpai, B.K. (eds.), *Community Participation in Natural Resource Management*, Rawat Publications, Jaipur and New Delhi, 2001.

Patnaik, B.K. and Brahmachari, A., *Economic and Political Weekly*, 1996.

Ramakrishna Mission Lokashiksha Parishad, West Bengal, "Environment Development Through People's Participation".

Ramakrishna Mission Lokashiksha Parishad, West Bengal, "Participatory Forest Management".

"Ruparel River Flows Again", Tarun Bharat Sangh, Bhikampur, Alwar (Rajasthan).

Shrotriya, Mohan, Aravali (NGO), Annual Report, 2000-2001.

"Watershed Development in Rajasthan: Activities and Achievements", Watershed Development and Soil Conservation Department, Government of Rajasthan, 2002.

5

Community Management of Tanks

In ancient India, there was a variety of community-managed irrigation systems. Water harvesting for agriculture was adopted in western India. The *Artha Shastra* of the Mauryan period refers to 'check dams' built for agriculture in Gujarat, which were renovated under King Ashoka in the 3rd century B.C. Some hillside check-dams in western India have remained under local management till the present times. Many other kinds of locally managed systems like tanks, khadins, baories, etc., for gathering and storing water can be found in arid regions of western and peninsular India. Attempts are being made to revive some of these systems and identify institutions for local community management in Gujarat, Kerala, Tamil Nadu, Punjab and elsewhere.

In India, large area is irrigated through tanks. Tamil Nadu has nearly 40,000 tanks irrigating one million hectares. In Karnataka, there is a record of tank construction since the 12th century. Now, there are 36,000 tanks. PWD controls the head sluice and the outlet, while the farmers maintain their field channels. Andhra Pradesh has about 70,000 tanks mostly constructed in mediaeval times. Maharashtra and Madhya Pradesh have about 4,000 each which were renovated later. In Himachal Pradesh, out of one lakh irrigated hectares, 70,000 hectares are managed by communal systems called 'Kuhals'. These are of ancient origin of utilizing hill streams for agriculture on community basis. Kings constructed tanks, etc., received one-sixth of the crop and handed over to local agencies for management and maintenance. Irrigation was managed by village sabhas (Tamil:*sabai*) or assemblies comprising of adult males of the village. In many cases, Gram Sabhas had tank supervision committees. One-third of the channels were closed for a time each year for maintenance. If money was required for maintenance, the panchayat would collect taxes from the farmers. During the British administration, irrigation became centralized.

Tank Irrigation in Andhra Pradesh

There are about 74,000 tanks in Andhra Pradesh which irrigate 1.2 million hectares amounting to nearly 26 per cent of the area under irrigation. Out of this 90 per cent tanks have a command of less than 40 hectares. Tanks are very useful in drought-affected area of Telangana and Rayalseema regions. Traditionally, tanks provide drinking water and were constructed during the 16th and 17th centuries by the then rulers. Tanks constructed by Vijay Nagar dynasty need special mention as after construction, the kings handed over subsequent management to the local community. Tanks are a classical case of community managed irrigation system in the country. It was tank water which, in fact, kept the villagers together. Though community management got a set-back during British regime but even today, people do involve themselves in the tank management. Positive effects of efficient water management and reduced cost of irrigation is still visible. No negative effects have been highlighted in studies done so far.

Tank water flows from the sluice into the distribution chamber from which major supply channels take off. Earthen channels are maintained by farmers before letting of the water. Informal committees are formed by the farmers for cleaning and maintaining the channels which involve silt removal, uprooting vegetation and strengthening the bunds. Members are chosen by consensus. Generally, educated people are preferred. Each member should be a good cultivator and normally from major communities like Reddis and Valmikis. Minor communities like Harijans, Chakala and Mangala do not find representation. The committee keeps a watch on water inflow into the tank and accordingly decides upon the time for opening the sluice. Before opening, the channels are cleaned under the supervision of the committee. Farmers committee appoints *neerugantis* (water manager) to attend to water distribution beneath the sluice. *Neerugantee* works under the supervision of the committees. He is paid in kind and cash.

Regarding maintenance, all farmers are expected to take part. Those who do not attend, are charged Rs. 25 per hectare and labourers are hired to do the cleaning. Thus, responsibility of maintenance rests with the village communities. Administrative control of the tanks is with the irrigation department.

Tank Irrigation in Karnataka

At present there are approximately 41,000 tanks in Karnataka. Tanks were constructed as early as in the 12th century. Most of the tanks are managed by Public Works Department (PWD). Farmers prefer to manage the affairs below the outlet.

Farmers organize an 'outlet committee' and prepare and implement the roster for the outlet for water distribution. Representatives from each outlet committees and local officials form a 'Tank Irrigation Committee'. Irrigation Management Committee (IMC) draws up the roster for distribution of water among the outlets. Outlet committee (OC) implements it below the outlet. PWD maintains main canal. Conflicts are resolved by farmers themselves in OC and IMC looking to nature of dispute. Communication between the farmers and departmental officers is very limited which needs to be developed for more efficient results. There is a need for more effective mechanism to ensure the adherence to the roster of water supplies providing access to all the farmers.

References

Clarence, Maloney and Raju, K.V., *Managing Irrigation Together*, Sage Publications, New Delhi, 1994.

Mishra, G.P. and Bajpai, B.K. (eds.), *Community Participation in Natural Resource Management*, Rawat Publications, Jaipur and New Delhi, 2001.

Satish, S. and Sundar, A., *People's Participation and Irrigation Management*, Commonwealth Publishers, New Delhi, 1990.

Uphoff, Norman, *Improving International Irrigation Management with Farmers' Participation*, Boulder Co., West View Press, 1986.

6

Community Participation in Irrigation Management

Though India has the largest irrigated area of any country in the world, there is a long history that irrigation is controlled by almost a single discipline – civil engineering. This has given the irrigation sector a technical perspective that only technical people can manage irrigation system. But, it has now been realized at central and state government levels too, that former emphasis on technology and construction should be broadened to deal with better water management, including farmers' management below some level. There is a trend of turn-over of irrigation systems to farmer management in many developing countries including Turkey, Mexico, Chile, Columbia, Indonesia, Egypt, Philippines, China, Morocco, Jordan, Albania, Yemen, Pakistan, Brazil, Indonesia and even countries like Nepal and Sri Lanka to a great extent. Some states in India, notably Maharashtra, too have started reorganizing irrigation. Himachal Pradesh, Andhra Pradesh, etc. National Water Policy in 1987 advocated 'participation' of farmers in management of irrigation systems. It said that "farmers should be involved progressively in various aspects of management of irrigation systems, particularly in water distribution and collection of water rates". This was encouraged by the

Government of India when it was laid down in the Eighth Five-Year Plan document that "the farmers can take over the maintenance and operation of the system themselves".

Since then, workshops were held almost in all states on 'Farmers Management in Indian Irrigation Systems'. The word 'participation' was dropped and the word 'management' was substituted. A National Policy Workshop was sponsored by the Central Water Commission (Patna, March 1992) after 18 such workshops. The Union Ministry of Water Resources also organized national level workshops subsequently in 1994, 1995, 1997 and 1999 on Participatory Irrigation Management.

Deficiencies

L.K. Joshi, Joint Secretary Ministry of Water Resources, Government of India, in his book *Irrigation and its Management in India*, summarized following deficiencies due to lack of appropriate irrigation water management:

- Water delivery is unreliable.
- Water distribution is inequitable and tail-end deprivation is almost universal. There is inadequate or no supply at tail-ends.
- Small farmers are also deprived of water due to indiscipline among farmers.
- Water use is very inefficient leading to over irrigation in part of command that leads to wastage of water. Lavish use of water also results in water logging and salinity as well as alkalinity.
- There is no group or individual incentive for farmers to conserve water and economize its use.
- Service to farmers is poor and marked by insensitivity due to bureaucratic apathy. Water users are entirely dependent on the staff of irrigation agency for the distribution of water. Their concern about adequacy of water, its timely delivery, regularity, for knowledge of amount of water to

be delivered, reduction of conflicts and equity in distribution of water are not the concerns of the staff of irrigation agency.

- Levy of water rates and recovery has no relation to actual cost of water, hence poor revenues and returns.
- There is inadequate maintenance and widespread deterioration of infrastructure.
- Excessive canal seepage.
- Insufficient drainage and water logging.
- Main system's deficiencies.
- Improper or mismatched cropping pattern and calendar.
- Water users have no role in administration of the system.
- Lack of information to the farmers about availability of water which hinders rational planning of crops.
- Non-provision of gauge measuring devices.
- Canals unable to carry designed discharge of water due to silting and damaged structures.
- Theft of water in sub-distributaries.
- Un-authorized outlets in some sub-distributaries.
- Field staff of irrigation department ineffective.
- Anarchy on canals and self-centred attitude of farmers.
- No system of allocation and distribution of water.
- Inequity between big and small farmers, head and tail enders. Bigger farmers are generally greater beneficiaries due to linkages between powerful social groups and unscrupulous officials.

"The approach is top-down. The prescriptions are handed from the top and irrigation is managed more according to standard administrative procedures than by local variable needs" as summarized by L.K. Joshi.

In view of the deficiencies noted above, the main recommendations were as under:

- Minor and community irrigation systems should be turned over completely to user groups.

- In medium and large systems, lower parts (outlet, minor canal, may be distributary) should be turned over to WUAs for management, water distribution, and maintenance; for user involvement higher in the system there need to be tiers or federations of WUAs.
- WUAs should distribute the water by rotation for equity.
- Planning should be by the agency and WUA together.
- Community organizers are required to be appointed for the social task of organizing farmers.
- WUAs should be formed at village or natural community level wherever possible. They should involve traditional rural institutions and also local and development administration.
- WUAs should be better registered as societies and have by-laws.
- Water should be delivered to WUAs on volumetric basis.
- WUAs should take over collection of water fees from farmers and transmit in an agreed proportion to the agency.
- Cropping pattern should be free.
- Conjuctive use of groundwater should be free.
- WUAs should be financially independent and raise their own funds from water fees, services, resources and contracts.
- WUAs should employ and pay their own watermen, watchmen, and technical specialists.
- The agency may make contracts with WUAs to undertake maintenance and improvements.

Role of Water Users

Norman Uphoff, in his book *Improving International Irrigation Management with Farmers' Participation,* described three phases of farmer's participation as under:

Phase I: Farmer as Water Receiver: Civil engineering was a principal requirement. Department's professional orientation was necessary. There was evolution in role and responsibility of water users. More concern was how to get water to the field in a fairly reliable way. Criterion was sufficiency rather than efficiency.

Phase II: Farmer as Water User: Farmers became more knowledgeable to raise returns from land. Agriculture and irrigation became productivity-oriented.

Phase III: Farmer as Water Manager: During this phase, role of farmer as water user should become much greater because farmer gains more knowledge about soils, pests, varieties, land preparation practices, optimum use of water and other inputs. Case for community participation becomes much stronger.

During this phase, the role of government agencies should also change from 'systems managers' to 'service providers'. Participation is there but nature of participation differs at different levels. The role of the community changes as under:

1. Acquisition of water during water sufficiency phase.
2. Allocation of water on equitable basis during operation phase.
3. Distribution of water for optimum results during operation of structures.
4. Drainage of water in case of excess supply.
5. Maintenance of structures for continued and efficient use of water.
6. Decision-making, resource mobilization, application of funds, manpower, materials and inputs, conflict resolution, communication of decisions regarding cropping pattern and optimum productivity, etc., are looked after by the community in the phase III.

State exercises control but more indirectly. It becomes 'wholesaler' instead of 'retailer' of water. Enabling atmosphere needs to be created for basic change in the mindset of the government departments concerned.

Objective

Community participation in water management should be genuine partnership between farmers and the government as a whole and not merely as an instrument for facilitating government schemes and programmes. Solving fiscal problem is not the goal. It should enable government to provide better services, efficient water delivery, more convenient operation of irrigation system, quick resolution of conflicts, etc., leading to higher and sustained productivity and also attract more resources from stakeholders for irrigation development. Farmer's direct involvement in system management as a compliment/substitute to state's role should be the basic objective. It is not privatization which refers to transfer of ownership to the agency but direct and effective involvement of beneficiaries in decision-making process.

Prerequisites

- *Water Scarcity*: If water is plenty, there is little need and reason to organize.
- *Poor Management*: Distribution of water to small farmers or at tail end should be the problem as a necessity to organize.
- *Smaller Groups*: They have stronger community ties and better inter-linkages to organize better and more effectively.
- *Social Background*: Common neighbourhood, common caste or religious ties, make enforcement of rules easier.
- *Full Flexibility*: Decision-making as per local needs.
- *O&M Grants*: In initial years, matching grants to WUAs will make them sustainable.
- *Training*: Capacity building is a must for success. Community organizers bring mass awareness among farmers, make attitudinal orientation of thinking and make them competent managers.

- *Multidisciplinary Teams*: It is not the civil engineers but multidisciplinary mobile teams for development of knowledge and skills of organization, agricultural management, suggest incentives, share experiences of other projects. They should be able to empower farmers as well as improve performance of programmes.

From Participation to Management

The idea that the farmers should 'participate' in irrigation management has grown in India since 1980s though formally adopted in National Water Policy, 1987 and the Eighth Plan. It has been driven by the need for more returns from the massive funds invested in irrigation, which has been a key factor in increasing agricultural production in India. There is a widespread feeling that investments have also not resulted in the anticipated benefits. Some even feel that many irrigation systems have caused damage to land resources through waterlogging, salinity, and even dislocation of poorer communities from hearth, home, soils and wells, etc., through submergence in big reservoirs which mainly benefited large farmers. Irrigation projects proved a disguised boon only. People's participation was fervently advocated by many sections of society.

Bureaucrats saw possible benefits in probable reduction in operating costs, specially in major and medium irrigation projects. Department was also interested in lightening their burden of maintenance, collection of water charges, etc. Department has also a view that a farmer has a tendency to waste water as value of water is not known to him.

Farmer's perspective is satisfaction of his genuine need for irrigating his fields. He wants equity in distribution of water if it is scarce, specially at the tail end. Hence, he wants Water Users Association (WUA). While none seem to object formation of water users associations, the crux lies in its orientation. Whether WUAs are to be formed to be used as tools by the government to fulfil its objectives or to develop them as a power base or to empower the community to take over management of water resources. It should come from below and not be imposed from above if people have to manage and be really empowered to take over operation and maintenance of the system. Participation is only advisory where decision-making power rests with the agency and not with the users. Hence, it is 'management' and not 'participation' which can really deliver the goods.

Participation does not mean that the farmers will only help and advise the government department to undertake assigned tasks but it should also mean that the irrigation agency feels accountable to farmers for providing required water at proper times for production purposes. Farmers are the chief clients who can take initiative for irrigation assessment, planning, management, equitable water distribution, collection of water charges, maintenance, etc. Farmers are not only the beneficiaries but the managers of the product (water) which they purchase and for which they pay to the supplier and be accountable. There should be no paternalistic attitude.

Development and donor agencies, such as IIMI, the Ford Foundation, USAID, the Netherlands government, European Economic Community (EEC), etc., have been sponsoring pilot projects of farmer management that the concerned beneficiaries should initiate, plan, manage and evaluate the effort of development. Beneficiaries should organize and manage by themselves right from the planning stage.

Characteristics of Community Management

1. Spontaneous support of the farmers under local leadership.
2. Structured role to play in management of the irrigation system.
3. Authority to make and implement decisions at appropriate levels.
4. Responsibility to raise its funds and manage its affairs.

Farmers of a WUA must feel a sense of ownership of the irrigation system and it is feasible only when they get control over it. In some countries like Mexico, Brazil or USA, WUAs manage whole irrigation systems, the managers and engineers are employed by them in water districts but in all the states of India, they are still employed by the government, so farmers seldom feel ownership and responsibility. Though it is difficult, but good water management requires cooperation by both. A relationship of mutual respect, with no 'gap' between irrigation officers and farmers.

By 1990s, in India, thousands of water user associations were formed in Maharashtra, but mostly they were on paper and generally failed in practice. They had no role in water management at higher levels, raised no funds for their affairs and were not seen as profitable by the farmers. Madhya Pradesh in the mid-1980s constituted Irrigation Panchayats under the Irrigation Act which remained as defunct organizations existing only on paper. In 1999, with the new legislation, 2,416 WUAs were constituted and elections held in April 2000. Election to Distributory Committees also were held in April, 2001. In Rajasthan, though the Act was passed in 2000, WUAs have been constituted as per a bottom up, flexible approach and registered as cooperative societies. Gujarat, Orissa, Uttar Pradesh, Haryana, Tamil Nadu and Karnataka are also the states using Cooperative Societies Act for WUAs. Demand driven WUAs are still rare and mostly they are governed by mandatory government orders. Moreover, they are mostly 'Chak Committees' in Canal Area Development (CAD) areas, on water courses below the canal outlet level and this cannot lead to participatory irrigation management (PIM) of canals.

Advantages of Community Management

Worldwide, the general experience is that successful WUAs bring many advantages as under:

1. *Advantages to Farmers*: Significant increase in crop yield, reduced conflicts among farmers, more reliable supply of

water, better water distribution, farmer's flexibility in use of water, choice of crops and land use, reduced gap between head and tail-end users, less waterlogging because of careful use of water and better resolution of conflicts and less opportunity for corruption and better mutual trust. Apart from these, farmers get fishing rights, income from sale of common resources like trees, grass, grazing, silt, etc. Experience has shown that participatory irrigation management (PIM), though not a panacea for all water management problems, can go a long way towards ensuring efficient running of canals, optimum on-field water application and re-use or proper drainage of the excess water from irrigation systems and farmers' fields – in short ensuring efficient land-water management.

2. *Advantages to Irrigation Officers and the Agency*: Improved relations with client farmers, reduced complaints of inequity, increase in irrigation efficiency, better water delivery, less mistrust, less burden of recovery and water distribution, etc. The government has less maintenance cost as a result of WUAs.
3. *Advantages to the State and the Nation*: Scarce water used more efficiently, higher yields, less waterlogging, economy in operational expenses of the department, reduced social costs, etc.

Conditions for Success of WUAs

There are 14 principles, which have been drawn from the working experience of India as well as other Asian countries leading towards success of working of WUAs. They could be summarized as under:

1. Farmers must take own initiative in assessment, planning, implementing and evaluating so that they find it useful and own them.
2. They should be genuine people's organizations and not paper WUAs created by government orders only. In such cases, they are bound to fail.

3. PLA attitude of bureaucrats is one of the pre-conditions. Talk less and listen more, be supportive rather than critical, be sympathetic to solving problems, provide all necessary information and guidance. Supportive and facilitative role of department is essential.
4. *Accountability to Water Users*: Relation of businessman and a customer needs to be developed. Attitude of benevolence of the government treating farmer as beneficiary has to be abandoned for success of WUAs.
5. *Role of Community Organizers*: Outside experts are necessary in the beginning to train members and develop a philosophy of managing water resources at community level.
6. *Quality of Local Leaders*: Much of the success will depend on the quality of decisions by the leaders regarding volume of water to be released to farmers, equitable distribution to farmers at tail end, proper water rates, proper maintenance with no scope for complaints of corruption.
7. *Flexibility*: Terms and conditions regarding price fixation, cropping pattern, other decisions are to left to the community rather than imposed from above. Discretion of participants should be honoured. They should be free to adopt internal decision-making systems. The Ninth Plan Working Group Reports in 1996 also contained recommendations in line with the flexible, bottom up and voluntary approach.
8. *Tiers of WUAs*: Large irrigation systems are difficult to run at the local level. Hence, WUAs have to be built upwards from the lowest ladder and gradually go to highest level. Management at lower levels can be more successful.
9. *WUAs Should be Sustainable Without Subsidies*: Experience has shown that initial subsidies for three years could not make WUAs sustainable. Expectation of subsidy develops a habit of dependence for ever, which should not be inculcated right from the beginning. For sustainability, they should undertake agriculture and allied activities also to

become independent of subsidies. It could be multi-disciplinary CAD organization.

10. *Environmental Protection*: Problems of waterlogging, salinity, chemical pollution, biomass, misuse of water, problems on tailenders, etc., can be looked into successfully only by WUAs rather than departmental officers. By mutual understanding and community decisions only, all these problems regarding environmental protection can be resolved.
11. *Intensive Capacity Building Effort*: In view of the past experience, proper capacity building of local leaders to share responsibility of management of scarce water resources must be taken up by the government through community leaders for running WUAs successfully.
12. *Human Engineering Effort*: Sincere effort for human resource development is a long term process as compared to construction of an irrigation dam. Organizational and social systems to develop will take time to work successfully, hence patience will be necessary to ensure success of WUAs.
13. *Water Management is Multidisciplinary*: Except civil engineers, agriculture experts to organize agriculture and cropping rotation, sociologists for PLA efforts and organize community, HRD experts should also work with WUAs for successful functioning.
14. *Mindset of Government Agencies need Reorientation*: All land and water resources of surface water, groundwater, watershed, wasteland development, Desert Development Programme (DDP), Drought Prone Aid Prone (DPAP) and the like are to be managed at local level through WUAs. Integrated development of land and water resources through local community is demand of the day as international agencies also desire and recommend.

Some Practical Experiences

K.K. Singh from an NGO in Hyderabad has narrated some experiences in his article, "The Story of PIM in India" after visiting PIM areas. He found that under government management, it is a common sight to see excessive seepage from canal banks, illegal tapping and pumping of water from canals. Upper reach farmers draw more water than their share even though downstream farmers within the irrigation command may not have seen the water for years. Less common but quite widespread is poor flow of water in minors and field channels due to defective design which is not rectified for years. Extensive cuts were noticed in the newly lined minors financed from World Bank loan under modernization programme.

At current prices, it costs more than Rs. 56,000 to bring one hectare under irrigation. Waste of water is nothing short of a criminal act and that too under the control of highly professional irrigation bureaucracy which is expected to safeguard the interests of a nation of small farmers. There should be no doubt about capability of the farmers for self-management.

- After visiting states in which *warabandi* or rotational water supply system was being implemented, he found that there was an agreement among the farmers that upstream farmers would draw water up to lunch and downstream farmers after lunch. If either of them fail, the villagers of the other area repair the cut and nobody would object. People were assured of sufficient water. Wherever canal supplies were poor, or the irrigation administration negligent or ineffective, individual farmers or groups take over the management in their hands. One point of interest under PIM was that wastage of water comes under control.
- In case of Paligunj distributory (Sone Command) of Bihar, there had been widespread lawlessness in water use. After farmers took initiative of managing over 12,000 hectares in 76 villages, over 90 per cent farmers were able to get command water whereas previously water could reach hardly in half the command area.

Andhra Pradesh

Indian Network on Participatory Irrigation Management (India NPIM) has been working on the subject. Andhra Pradesh was the first state to enact Andhra Pradesh Farmers' Management of Irrigation Systems Act, 1997 and covered all irrigation schemes - major, medium and minor - under 10,292 WUAs and 174 Distributory Committees. Farmers' willingness to undertake PIM is essential pre-condition for the sustainability of PIM, provided returns from PIM provide reasonable incentives to compensate against costs of managerial responsibilities:

1. Irrigation system up to a minor or group of minors covering a command area of 750 hectares or more are placed under WUA. Farmers manage irrigation system in their area.
2. WUAs are autonomous bodies which function on democratic lines so as to function effectively.
3. Agreement between WUA and the agency is signed to enable independent functioning of the farmer.
4. WUA is responsible for maintenance and operation of irrigation network in its area.
5. Agency will make available assured and reliable water at head of minors to WUA and undertake rehabilitation and modernization of distribution system and facilitate recovery of maintenance charges from users.
6. WUA will be at liberty to regulate distribution of water to water users on volumetric basis or any other basis and to levy and collect penalties for the system under its management.
7. WUA will be at liberty to save water by improving efficiency of irrigation system and make water so saved available to users on payment.

Pilot projects showed very encouraging results. Area irrigated increased from pre-project level of about 50 per cent to 80 per cent with the same quantity of water as was supplied in earlier years and without any substantial investment on rehabilitation or repairs of the system.

Though 90 per cent water charges are to be given to WUAs but water charges have increased from Rs. 150 to Rs. 500 per hectare after 1 April 1997. There are no clear cut water rights to farmers, work of recovery of water rates or quantity of water to be delivered to WUA find no place in agreements.

Capacity building of the WUAs is being done through a series of training programmes. It is a continuous process of training at the grassroots level the farmers and government functionaries of revenue, irrigation and agriculture departments in skills in managing the irrigation systems, writing the accounts, negotiations and dispute resolutions. Open dialogue between farmers and government departments takes place to remove difficulties. In spite of strong political will of the Chief Minister, it requires a highly committed political and administrative will to make it successful.

Bihar

WALMI, Patna initiated the action research pilot project of Paliganj Distributory in Sone Command which is a successful example of community irrigation in Bihar. Before taking up the project, there was complete indiscipline, head-end farmers commonly breached the canal, there was no maintenance, there were social tensions due to caste factions and officials did not dare to visit the area since incensed farmers attacked them. Effort was made in March 1989 when Distributory Canal Committee of 35 members was formed by farmers and village level irrigation committees were initially formed in 20 villages (5-9 members of different castes and tenures) one from every village. The committee focused on distribution of water and agricultural activities around canal command. It closed breaches, removed stop logs, set up rotational arrangement along the canal. There were 20 farmers who monitored the operation. They collected water rates, deposited 30 per cent to the irrigation department and kept 70 per cent for operation and maintenance by the committee. Physical condition of the canal improved. Water became available to farmers in lower reaches and it resulted in better crops. The unique experiment was successful.

Three more pilot projects, including Jamunia branch of Gandak Project, were also taken up in other command areas. Operation was handed over to farmers. Paliganj pilot project was of course the most successful.

Goa

Pipe Committees were formed in CAD areas. In all, 36 water distribution cooperatives were registered. *Warabandi* is looked after by a society. Societies collect water charges and keep only 10 per cent margin for working capital. Government pays at the rate of Rs. 5 per metre for maintenance of water course and reimburses salary of the canal supervisor. The societies work as agents of the state. They have no water rights. Power to decide conflicts rests with the canal officer. Canal officer can even stop water to the society. Thus, there is no farmers' management in practice in Goa.

Gujarat

Mohini Cooperative Society of Ukai Kakrapar dam on Taki river is often quoted as pilot experiment of community management. In a command of 466 hectares, hardly 120-160 hectares could get water, though there was no shortage of water but some farmers obstructed water. Distribution system was defective; irrigation department was silent. Initiative of one farmer, Bhiku Bhai prepared farmers to form a cooperative in 1977-78 though the dam was constructed in 1971. But, since no institution was there, the society could not sustain itself, although initially it ran successfully due to cleaning of canals and proper distribution of water.

WUA in Mahi-Kadana command was also successful during the first two years when farmers cooperated and were sensible in using water. But slowly they reverted to old habits. All could not get water. Therefore, 13 pilot projects were started. WUAs take water from the department, distribute water to farmers, collect water charges, carry out maintenance, and resolve conflicts. WUA keeps 50 per cent of collection for maintenance and as collection charges. There is favourable atmosphere for participation of NGOs; also in Gujarat community organizers of NGOs motivate and train the farmers The number of NGOs is also very much limited. Except 13 cooperatives, there are 283 *mandalies* (User Associations) covering 36,000 hectares in the command area of various irrigation projects but they are formed in isolated portions of canal system and have no linkage even in the same canal area. Progress of involvement of NGOs as well as integrated community participation is very slow.

Haryana

Participatory irrigation management was taken up in Kaimri minor on Devsar feeder in Bhakra canal command in Hissar (106 farmers), Khera sub-minor on Pheowa minor of Markanda distributory in Kurukshetra (335 farmers) and 725 WUAs were registered but all was at water course level only and after the outlet. Work done was not encouraging so far as community irrigation management is concerned.

Himachal Pradesh

In olden times, there were *kuhls* which provide excellent example of management by community which ran quite successfully without state support. In Kangra valley, 30,000 hectares are said to have been irrigated on community basis. *kuhls* were constructed without state patronage and responsibility for managing each *kuhl* rested with farmers. Annual repairs and maintenance was also carried out by communal parties and supervised by *Kohli* (water master). Gradually, there was decline in the system because of tensions in management. Conflicts between head and tail farmers increased; *Kohli* could not enforce customary rules and government intervened to take over the work of *Kohli.* Some farmers' associations were formed initially but have become defunct by now.

Karnataka

One NGO formed WUA in 1980 in Malaprabha command and CAD department motivated farmers to form 49 cooperative societies but due to non-cooperation of the irrigation department, it could not function. The Ghoshal Committee suggested for community participation in irrigation management in 1996 but no further action has perhaps yet been taken. The committee suggested that WUA may levy and collect water charges and retain 20 per cent and pass on the rest to the government. Maintenance funds with government may be passed on to WUAs. But, the intention appears to be to keep WUA as agents of the state rather than managers of irrigation system.

Kerala

Though 3-tier farmer associations at outlet, canal and project level are contemplated but as yet there are no special achievements of community management in the state. Beneficiary farmer's association have been given the responsibility of distribution of water below the outlet. Main function of the committee is to ensure that water is distributed equitably in all areas of the project. Provisions do exist but no example of community management is worth quoting.

Madhya Pradesh

Act was framed in July 1999 on the lines of Andhra Pradesh. There were 64 societies registered to work as 'water panchayats'. But they were powerless and lacked direction. It is proposed to entrust operation and maintenance to WUAs up to minor level, recovery of irrigation dues and conflict resolution to farmers as per provisions of the new Act. No example of community participation of irrigation management is worth quoting.

Maharashtra

Small-scale irrigation system managed by the community was prevalent in Maharashtra in 17th century known as *'phad'* system. Management was done entirely by irrigators with no involvement of the irrigation department. In 1947, Pani Panchayats were set up to enable farmers to participate in irrigation management, though role of Pani Panchayats was only advisory.

Pilot project for management of a minor on the right bank canal of Mula irrigation system was started in 1987. Society was registered in 1989 when it took over water management and repairs below the minor. Three societies – Ban Ganga, Mahatma Phule and Jai Yogeshwar – were organized by the efforts of Bapu Upadhyaye in 1991 on sub-minors of Waghad right bank canal. Management committee of 14 farmers for each society constructed dams also and managed water distribution including collection of water fee. WUAs could determine water rates and need not necessarily follow the government rates. Disputes were resolved by the committee consisting of nominee of WUA, irrigation department and executive engineer of the cell. Decision of committee is binding on both sides. Rs. 20 per hectare is handed over to WUA for maintenance of the system. Technical help of the department is provided to WUAs. An amount of 10 per cent of the grant for O&M is passed on to WUAs for rehabilitation of the system. NGOs have been making efforts to organize farmers to form WUAs and take over management of irrigation system on above lines. Water and Land Management Institute (WALMI),

Aurangabad has developed a sound capacity building programme for training of farmers and officials in community participation in irrigation management. The work is proceeding slowly, perhaps due to absence of legal back up and lack of motivation among officials of the department. There are defunct WUAs also and there is no turnover as yet.

Orissa

Action research was initiated on Mahanadi Delta Irrigation Project and outlet level associations were formed. A joint management phase has been introduced to familiarize the farmers with technical matters in four projects. Community management of irrigation system is yet to take shape.

Punjab

No effort has been initiated due to *warabandi* (rotational water supply) system already in practice in the state.

Rajasthan

Chak Samitis in IGNP area and Catchment Committees in Chambal command area were formed in the beginning for on-farm development activities but they languished in due course of time since they had no defined functions. Before 1995, Water Distribution Committees consisted of officials and elected representatives where water users had no say. *Warabandi* for drawing water from the water course was in vogue like Punjab. Farmers manage to operate the water distribution schedule below the outlet.

After 1995 also, WUAs were registered in Chambal CAD project area but unfortunately many CAD officers have viewed partnership of farmers as an instrument for getting government programmes implemented. Chak Samitis get government funds to take up government works like silt clearance from canals or water courses or take government work on contract basis.

Government policy is there that wherever operation, maintenance and management of canals would be done by WUAs themselves, cost per hectare for such works not exceeding Rs. 3,000 could be spent of which 10 per cent is contributed by WUA. But community management to enable WUA as sustainable managers of their irrigation systems is still not in practice.

Tamil Nadu

There is a long tradition of tank irrigation on community basis and there are about 39,000 tanks in the state. Management of irrigation water from Distribution Channel System below the head sluice is sole responsibility of farmers. Farmers provide free labour for maintenance known as *'kudimaramat'*. It is in vogue in all irrigation tracts of Tamil Nadu. But, the system has failed in recent times.

In CAD areas, some societies were registered but most of them are pipe (outlet) committees. Community organizers were also recruited to organize the farmers. Associations were formed but at sluice level generally commanding 20-30 hectares. Effort has been made to form farmers' councils at the distributory level and also an apex committee federating farmers' associations. Legal enactment for community management of irrigation system is yet to be implemented.

Uttar Pradesh

The Uttar Pradesh government in 1999 has transferred 29,000 deep tubewells to panchayats which will manage them through WUAs. Society bears the cost of electricity and appoints a tubewell operator for running it. It ensures equitable distribution of water including farmers belonging to scheduled castes as per study of Mampur by Niranjan Pant. Participatory irrigation management has been made a major policy instrument.

West Bengal

West Bengal is a good example of community water management in tubewell irrigation system. There are 3,000 high capacity tubewells in the state. Before handing over to panchayats there was vandalism and theft. Water rates were very low. For effective operation and maintenance, a cluster of 6-7 tubewells after energization were handed over to panchayats. Gram Panchayats organized beneficiary committees and gave them responsibility for operating and maintaining the system. One Sabhapati, one representative of beneficiaries and one representative of panchayat run the system successfully. They have power to fix rates to meet the operation costs.

Community water management has reduced incidence of theft, developed a sense of ownership among farmers, water rates are economical, decisions are taken promptly, there is optimum utilization of installed capacity, local operator gets employment and uses water effectively, cost of O&M is reduced, repairs are promptly attended by local mechanics, and appropriate cropping pattern is adopted after discussions among farmers. It is a successful experiment of community water management.

Thus, the experience of various states indicates that tubewells irrigation management in West Bengal or Uttar Pradesh is comparatively successful. In pilot projects there was initial success but community management on sustainable basis are yet an exception. A climate is yet to be built for changing the mindset of irrigation officials and community organizers have to create an initiative and build capacity among farmers to take over management of irrigation systems in times to come. Legal enactments alone may not be the way forward.

References

Clarence, Maloney and Raju, K.V., *Managing Irrigation Together*, Sage Publications, New Delhi, 1994.

Hooja, Rakesh and Joshi, L.K. (eds.), *Participatory Irrigation Management*, Volume I & II, Rawat Publications, Jaipur and New Delhi, 2000.

Hooja, Rakesh, Pangare, Ganesh and Raju, K.V., *Users in Water Management*, Rawat Publications, Jaipur and New Delhi, 2002.

Satish, S. and Sundar, A., *People's Participation and Irrigation Management*, Commonwealth Publishers, New Delhi, 1990.

Uphoff, Norman, *Improving International Irrigation Management with Farmers' Participation*, Boulder Co., West View Press, 1986.

7

Community Watershed Management

It is a known fact that two-thirds of the earth's surface is covered by water and only one-third surface is land. Unfortunately, 97.2 per cent of this natural water resource exists in the form of salty water in the sea whereas 2.2 per cent water is frozen at the North and South Poles in the form of snow. Approximately remaining less than 1 per cent of water resource which is recycled in nature, is used by man. Ever increasing population and its ever increasing physical necessities go on reducing per capita availability of water for mankind. In view of scarcity of water, one cannot think of sustainability of land and human beings. Sustainable human development not only generates economic growth but distributes its benefits equitably, that regenerates the environment rather than destroying it, that empowers people rather than marginalizing them. If groundwater is pumped out for agriculture by rich farmers and by the government for drinking purposes through tube wells, small and marginal farmers have to bank upon only rain water. It is estimated that hardly 28 per cent of rain water is used through dams and canals whereas 72 per cent goes waste by flowing in rivers and nallahs. The only alternative is to harness such rain water for the poor farmers specially in drought areas, arid and semi-arid areas to save the most important natural resource of land and water. In view of the ever increasing seriousness of the problem of land-water environment, implementation of water and land conservation programmes at community level on a war footing has become an imminent necessity.

To obtain the optimum production of biomass, all the three natural resources of soil, vegetation and water have to be managed efficiently. One has to look for a suitable unit of management so that these resources are managed effectively, collectively and simultaneously. Water can be managed efficiently only if a watershed is taken as a unit. Since soil and vegetation can also be conveniently and efficiently managed in this unit, the watershed is considered an ideal unit for managing three vital and interdependent natural resources of soil, water and vegetation. The watershed approach is being increasingly used in various development programmes like soil and water conservation, erosion control, command area development, rainfed farming, ravine reclamation and waste land development.

Watershed Defined

A watershed is a natural geohydrological entity. It is an area, the run off from which drains through a pre-determined single outlet on the drainage system. It is an aerial expanse of the land surface from which the run off flows through a defined drain, channel, stream or river. Its synonyms are 'catchment area' and 'drainage basin'. The boundaries of a watershed are known as drainage divide, precipitation on opposite sides of drainage divide falls into different watersheds. Obviously, there are hierarchies of streams that flow into each other as tributaries. Likewise, there are hierarchies of watersheds that may be micro (a few hectares) for a small stream up to macro (hundreds of thousands of km) for a large river system. Only part of the precipitation that falls on a watershed ultimately gets into the stream – it is known as run off and varies widely among watersheds. The rest of the precipitation either evaporates back into the atmosphere (directly or indirectly) or soaks into the ground (percolation or infiltration). The part of the precipitation that is intercepted by vegetation is also evaporated and returned to the air. Out of the water that soaks into the ground, part is absorbed by roots or plants and returned to atmosphere by transpiration.

The All India Soil and Land Survey Organization has delineated watersheds on the basis of region, basin, catchment, sub-catchment, watershed, sub-watershed, milli-watershed, micro-watershed and mini-watershed. For land management purposes, a convenient size of watershed is about 500 to 1,000 hectares but the limits cannot be taken rigidly since it is a geographical unit depending on the catchment of water in a particular area. Proper land management needs cooperation of the community and active participation of the farmers whose lands fall therein for planning, execution and subsequent maintenance of the project, boundaries of concerned revenue village or Gram Panchayat are also to be kept in view.

Watershed Management

Watershed management envisages systematic and scientific approach towards conservation, harvesting, proper utilization and safe disposal of flowing water from the moment it falls on the land surface in the form of rain. For the protection of our natural resources like land, water, vegetation and livestock and their development programmes, watershed is taken as a unit of development rather than an administrative or revenue unit. Soil conservation Acts existing almost in all the States are devoted to the management of land, water, pasture lands and forests. These Acts require people to evolve their own small field projects with the help of soil conservation personnel. Majority support of the people is necessary before the project can be launched. In practice, people's participation has been more on paper than in reality. Even NGOs working with foreign funds, enlist support of people in advisory capacity rather than as planners, executors and decision-makers of the project proposals. Consulting the people, rather than involving them in decision-making, has been the general practice of the government departments. Strong and effective farmer's groups are the foundation and central feature of successful watershed development programmes.

New State Policy

Towards the end of 1994, Hanumanthaiya Committee appointed by the Government of India recommended:

1. Water conservation and not soil conservation is the most important. Water holds key for development of rainfed areas. If water is conserved, soil would be conserved automatically.
2. Unless sizeable areas are treated and developed, ecological benefits like control of siltation of reservoirs, rejuvenation of eco-systems in drought prone and desert areas, mitigation of the effects of weather aberrations, improvements in the productivity of rainfed lands, etc., would not accrue.
3. It is impossible to treat sizeable areas without adopting low cost and yet effective technologies.
4. It is also impossible to cover the problem areas in foreseeable future through the government machinery/ set-up. Necessarily the projects will have to be planned, implemented and maintained through active and willing participation of the people.
5. There will be community participation in soil and water management only when they perceive direct and tangible benefits for themselves and understand technology.
6. The full participation of the watershed committees may be facilitated when the programme is built up on their accumulated wisdom, skills and systems. The complicated technologies imposed from outside inhibit willing participation of the local people.

New approach of participatory natural resource management would enthuse the people, make the development programmes really useful for the local people, and make them come forward to welcome and participate in the great national venture towards sustainable management of the natural resources to produce abundance for our growing population without damaging the resource base. Basic changes envisage:

- A typical rainfed farmer derives his livelihood from his small landholding, his/her share from community lands and by rearing livestock. Therefore, farming system development approach is indispensable.
- Landless and marginal farmers exercise tremendous impact on non-arable lands and vegetation thereupon, for fuel, fodder and collection of medicinal and utility materials. Unless rural poor-landless, artisans and marginal farmers are included as beneficiaries, watershed development projects would have little chances of sustainable development.
- Livestock play a crucial role in degeneration/regeneration of vegetation, particularly on common grazing grounds. A livestock component should be included in all the projects.
- Rural poor are engaged in one or other biomas based cottage industry for income generation. Such activities should invariably be included in watershed development projects.
- The project has to focus on a multi-disciplinary approach to watershed development. It is an integrated programme of soil conservation, water conservation, construction of water storing structures, flood water storage, contour bunding, check dams, terraces, gully control, diversion channels, grassed waterways, farm ponds, water harvesting structures like anicuts and nalla bunding, developing surface and ground water resources, efficient water use management, livestock development, pasture development, agro forestry, tree plantation, fodder development.

Dairy development, agricultural development, horticulture, women development, employment generation through self-help groups of poorer sections of the community.

- Instead of government projects with people's participation, they should be people's projects with government participation. People's participation has to be ensured throughout the project cycle.
- Training will be given to farmers on participation, managing and working of groups of beneficiaries and technical matters related to crop production and soil and moisture conservation practices. Women farmers will have a high priority while selecting trainees and project will make full use of their experience wherever possible.
- It will ensure sustainable management of natural resources because the community watershed committee will not only plan and execute but also maintain the assets after completion of the project period.
- Beneficiaries would contribute at least 10 per cent of the project expenditure which will remain deposited as 'Development Fund' to be utilized for maintenance after the completion of the project, over a period of five years.
- All the development expenditure is placed at the disposal of the local committee which prepares the account under the guidance of the WDT who verify its genuineness and committee submits it to the sanctioning authority. Indigenous technical knowledge of the community is to be utilized compulsorily rather than modern techniques. Local cheap material has to be used on priority.
- A high degree of flexibility and targeting of location-specific problems in project planning and implementation is required.
- Priority is given to panchayats for implementation of the watershed projects.

- Women, SC, ST, panchayat members are also to be included in the Watershed Committee to ensure their participation and empower them through decision making in development of the village.

Thus, it is realized that if development programmes are to be sustainable and their benefits are to reach the targeted group, a basic prerequisite is that the people, for whom these programmes are designed, must be involved in the planning and implementation of these programmes. A key factor towards this change was the increasingly widespread recognition that repeated failures have plagued many development programmes mainly because they were designed and implemented by outside development experts, with no beneficiary or target group involvement. Evidence has built up to demonstrate that that where people and their wishes and priorities are not put first, projects that affect and involve them, face problems. Experience, also shows, conversely, that where people were consulted, where they participate freely, where their needs and priorities are given primacy in project identification, design, implementation and monitoring, then economic and social performance are better and development is more sustainable. Leaving aside other influencing factors, in rural development, 'putting people first' is a necessary condition for good performance. People's involvement is specially necessary for the highly complex land and water resource based watershed development projects.

Role of the Government

- Government would provide 90 per cent finance towards cost of the project at the rate of Rs. 5,000 per hectare for integrated development of the area.
- Salary of secretary of watershed committee appointed at the local level would be borne out of such grant.
- Honorarium of Rs. 200 per month each for two volunteers to assist the secretary in women development, livestock

development and other activities will also be borne out of the government grant.

- A WDT consisting of a social scientist, agricultural graduate, veterinary graduate and an engineer would be available to the community for technical guidance in the respective fields.
- Administrative expenses to the extent of 10 per cent of the project expenditure can be spent out of the government grant as honorarium to WDT members and salary of secretary.

Steps in Participatory Management

1. *Site Selection*: Farmers in the area select the site suffering from soil erosion due to hilly terrain from where rain water runs off with great speed due to sloping terrain and harms their fields. With its focus on land, watershed development is biased towards those who own it, hence involvement of owners of land right from the start is essential.
2. *Identification of Beneficiaries*: Affected people form a group, select their team to plan and execute the project for optimum land utilization, water conservation, vegetative cover and maximizing production from fields, pastures and livestock. It is essential that all groups in the village participate in the planning of activities to be taken up, so that while 'putting people first, we also ensure that we put the last first'.
3. *Formulate a Plan*: After assessment of land, water, forestry, livestock and other natural and human resources, submit a proposal for sanction.
4. *Sanction of the Project*: Based on watershed maps prepared on the basis of imageries received from the satellite, area is finalized by the sanctioning agency. Rs. 5,000 per hectare is the standard rate out of which 10 per cent can be spent on administration, 5 per cent on survey, 5 per cent on

training and community works and 80 per cent on development works.

5. *Survey*: Area is got surveyed for contour bunding as per slopes, water harvesting structures, earthen check dams, flood control bunds, nalla bunding, erosion control measures, pasture development etc.
6. *Super-Imposition of Survey Map on Revenue Map*: Locate the site of works on Khasra map of revenue department
7. *Training and Community Works*: Members of WDT and Watershed Committee (WC), secretary and volunteers are trained so as to handle the project execution jobs. Confidence of the community is won by 'Entry-Point Activities' to involve cooperation of members by organizing the community in youth clubs, repair of schools or temples as urgently needed by the community, digging of hand pumps to solve immediate problem of drinking water at strategic points, etc.
8. *Identify Problems and Technological Options*: As per local problems, identify solutions based on indigenous technical knowledge. If interventions in watershed development are to be sustainable and replicable, we must work towards locally acceptable solutions, which again require that the project invests time and effort in enlisting beneficiary participation. Unless all affected persons of the whole watershed area are brought together to enable a joint understanding of the problems faced and suggested solutions, any interventions that attempt to improve the productivity of land will give rise to conflict situations that will undermine the objectives of productivity, sustainability and equity, central to watershed projects.
9. *Prepare Estimates*: Prepare physical and financial proposals.
10. *Activity Scheduling.*
11. *Execution of Plan by Various Farmer Beneficiary Groups*: It is the beneficiaries who are responsible for execution of the project activities so that they own the project and care

for its sustenance in future also, since their share is also invested in it in the form of cash, material or labour.

12. *Monitoring and Supervision*: It is the WC members who meet jointly at intervals to review and monitor progress of activities. Individually also, the committee members are responsible for supervision on site during execution of activities and Gram Sabha of beneficiaries have occasion for social audit during annual or six monthly meetings. After two years, Gram Sabha re-elects the members of WC to ensure responsive and accountable committee of the community who should work with transparency.
13. *Maintenance*: Since the benefits of watershed development projects are not confined only to the project duration period, but continue to accrue to the area and its people after the project has been technically completed, it is essential that that the people's institutions are established that are able to sustainably manage and distribute equitably the benefits of a watershed development project. Sustainability itself implies that the community would manage all its assets, natural and human resources to meet the demand for increasing long-term wealth and well-being without decreasing over time.

Participatory Learning and Action (PLA)

How to involve community in development projects? For this PLA methodology was evolved because 'top-down-pre-planned-package-model' of development had been frustrating to put up with. These seemed to work as long as the project was in operation due to external intervention but collapsed with withdrawal of the project. Where had the failure occurred? Was the planning wrong? Were inadequate backward and forward linkages the problem? "How do we get the people to participate in our programmes?" is an oft asked question by many sincere workers. The question itself embodies the answer. It is not 'them' participating in 'our' programmes but 'us' participating in their programmes. It advocates that the people themselves are 'solution agents' for their problems. It cuts down the 'normal professional bias' and anti-poverty bias towards people. It also reduces down the normal time consuming long methods of survey which consumes the much needed resources and that gives results after a long time. PLA is cost-effective, accurate and timely. The paradigm shift basically involves reversal attitude to learning from the community. The changed attitude to learning from the community facilitates recognizing their intelligence and efforts to forge out a survival strategy to ensure survival in the adverse circumstances of their environment. Understanding and appraising this time tested effort to control and survive in this environment, facilitates a consorted Village Resource Development plan, designed and developed by the community itself, to bring about development.

We have too often adopted an attitude of acting as if we know everything about everything. The result of this is that as soon as we get to the community, we start trying to teach them instead of listening and learning. Laying a heavy emphasis on unlearning before learning from the community is sometimes misunderstood by sceptics who think it a glorification of 'native wisdom'.

There are three specific areas in which attitudinal reverses have to occur:

1. In our attitude to learning
2. In our attitude to being open
3. In our attitude to seeing things differently

Learning

Developing the right attitude to learning has a prerequisite and that is recognizing that the community knows more about itself than we do. Since they were born in that environment and have continued to struggle in it, it stands to reason that they are the ones who know their own environment best. Recognizing this helps us to be interested, be curious and ask questions with genuine interest.

Being Open

Being open basically means not trying to bulldoze our priorities on to the community. It means listening to them even when their priorities might be quite different from that we thought they were. It also means facilitating those who cannot read and write to speak out. It involves making special efforts to make weaker, marginalized and oft overlooked people express themselves.

Seeing Things Differently

By overcoming biases on personal preferences and our presumptive, elitist, educational arrogance, we can succeed in PLA. To do this successfully one has to learn how to ask open ended questions like: Who? What? When? How? Where? And what else? The more one asks the more one learns. Once we are able to affect this crucial reversal in attitude we are able to learn from the community and with openness 'see things differently... for a change', the way the community does.

Preparing the Community

Preparing the community, before a PLA exercise is conducted, is very important particularly since a great deal of interaction takes place in a short period of time and the open ended questions can easily result in a false raising of hopes. The organizers should therefore try to convene a brief meeting of the community including opinion leaders among them and explain that the purpose of the entire exercise is to learn from the community about their ways and their background. They should be explained that the team that intends to come into the community to carry out PLA exercises consists of people who are from various disciplines and seek to learn about the community. The community should therefore concentrate on sharing information about themselves rather than wasting time on asking for new things or programmes. Care should also be taken to ensure that the community is not busy during that time with preparations for or celebration of any festival or sowing or harvesting season. Careful timing so as not to clash with local village markets (Which are generally held weekly) is also essential to ensure that the maximum number of community members are available for interaction.

Techniques

Several simple and interesting techniques can be used in PLA methodology to get to know the community well. There are about 40 known exercises that can be conducted and several new ways of conducting these have also emerged from time to time. One must, however, remember that a great deal of flexibility exists in using such semi-structured interactive interviewing techniques. Hence, PLA exercises should be used as per circumstances and availability of time.

PLA exercises can be listed as under:

- Time Line
- Family Line
- Trend Analysis
- Seasonality Diagramming
- Pie Diagram
- Participatory Resource Mapping
- Transects
- Matrix Ranking
- Chappati Diagram
- Wealth (or well being) Ranking
- Causal Diagrams
- Profile of Women's Work Day
- One Page Story
- Village/Community Resource Development Plan
- Conflict Analysis
- Water Resource and Use Pattern

- Commercial Activity in The Community
- Cattle Disease and Local Treatment Techniques

Time Line

The purpose of time line is to get a sort of historical review of the community and find out major events which have impact on community. People generally remember the things that have affected them. It serves as a good 'ice breaker' if conducted at the beginning of the programme, as community members love to share about their village and 'tell stories' of early events.

Method generally adopted is that the older people in the community including women are first contacted for this and after rapport building they are asked certain preliminary questions like, how their village got its name, who were the first inhabitants, where they came from? Care is taken to ask open-ended questions and not to interrupt the interviewees when they start responding. As the interview progresses, more people join in and start chipping in information. As they get on sharing information, the community is asked to share what were the major events that took place in their area and they are also asked to say "approximately when" it happened. Since exact time cannot be remembered by members, it will have to be estimated by the age of the person when it happened correlating to his present age.

Events could be like construction of road, starting of bus service, opening of primary school, installation of hand pump or water supply system, small pox, any epidemic, hospital, spread of disease, heavy rains or floods, famine years, panchayat election, electrification, etc

Expected Output

The information collected helps in understanding the community, their background, and the circumstances that affected them. It also indicates how they faced the adverse situations.

Family Line

This exercise is conducted to find out how the events and circumstances existing in the village have affected a few sample individual families.

Method

A mix of old, middle aged and young people is selected. After rapport building, one of them, preferably an older person is asked to trace his or her ancestors as far back as can be remembered. Coming down the family line from there, we find out how many children were born to this person, what happened to them, whom they married, what they did for a living and so on, till the present generation. All relevant information like undertaking of business, agriculture, migration, education, service employment, etc., is noted down. A lot of participation is generated in this exercise and soon many volunteers want to share information about their families too.

Expected Output

As one studies the family line, particularly comparing it with the time line of the village, one is able to see how people coped with and countered or adopted to certain stress situations. The overall result on outsiders is a sense of appreciation for the heritage of the community, its culture, its traditions and its survival instinct.

Trend Analysis

The purpose is to identify how trends of change in the community help us to understand how things have been changing in various fields over an approximate given time. An analysis of this trend indicates the overall direction in which the community is moving.

Method

Contact is made with a mix of young and old people and after establishing rapport with them, they are asked to identify what major changes have taken place in their community over a period of time. The older people are asked to recall how things were, when they were children and what they notice as the change now. The information is picturised in an easily understandable way using diagrams or symbols that the community themselves draw. This exercise can be done to study the trends of change in health care, immunization, diseases and their treatment, education, girls education, dowry and no dowry, size of the family, livelihood, house construction pattern, borrowing from money lenders, saving attitudes or no savings, cultivation, eating patterns, clothing, etc.

Expected Output

This change of trend in recallable lifetime shows the response of the people to changing circumstances by way of adaptation or modification in their attitudes and actions. The overall trends of the community show which direction they are moving in and what new changes are likely to be acceptable to them.

Seasonality Diagramming

Most of the activities in the village follow a set pattern which is determined by the season. Hence, the purpose of this method is to get wide range of information in a seasonal perspective.

Method

To initiate the thinking process in a favourable direction one begins with asking the mixed group of community members to identify different months of the year. The same names and starting month identified by them are used and further reference is made to the same names. The group is asked to show the months represented in a linear fashion using 12 stones, using one stone for each month. They are then asked to show the months during which there is rainfall, using seeds and placing these in quantity to show intensity of rainfall against the representative month. Once this is done, they are asked to use other seeds or small stones to show the seasonality of agriculture, work load, disease incidence, festival seasons, seasons of income, loan requirements, etc. Soon a comprehensive diagram showing the seasonality of occurrences of various events emerges. A visual model that can be understood and discussed by all young and old irrespective of whether they are educated or not, is drawn.

Expected Output

This is a very versatile exercise that can be used for discussing a wide range of issues. It can particularly be used to identify crisis periods in the community when outside intervention is required. It can become the basis for discussion regarding the introduction of new programmes or modification of unsuitable ongoing ones.

Pie Diagrams

Pie diagrams are used to find out the percentage distribution of various components compared to the whole. For example pie diagrams can be prepared for land use pattern, livelihood analysis, crop share, etc.

Method

This exercise works well with most groups as long as they understand the purpose of the exercise. For example if one is to prepare a pie diagram of the livelihood of the source of the community, this could be a useful diagram. There could be many sources of income differing in different seasons. One asks the group to imagine that all the income from various sources throughout the year is converted into money and placed in one place. If this is imagined one rupee = 100 paise, then how many paise come from different sources. The group soon understands and a pie diagram emerges showing the different segments representing different sources of income.

Expected Output

The importance of various components in terms of the larger percentage chunks helps in identifying which are more important sources for development.

Participatory Resource Mapping

The purpose is to obtain an overview of the resources available with the community in the form of social, economic, demographical and geographical details of the area where the community lives.

Method

A suitable central place is located where a large group can assemble. The community members are asked to draw out their village on the ground using colour powders and other locally available materials. They are asked to imagine how their village or settlement would look to a bird flying over the village and then draw it out showing all the various resources like roads, houses, fields, forests, hills, ponds, fields etc. The facilitators should make it a point not to direct what is to be presented and how, but just keep asking questions about each of the drawings. As they keep asking, the map becomes more and more detailed and often has nothing missing. School, dispensary, panchayat, patwar ghar, market, bazar, handpump and other social service institutions should be depicted in social mapping including mohallas along with names of communities which reside there. Different colours may be used for indicating different resources, eg., green for trees, grey for fields, blue for water, and the like.

Expected Output

Once the resource map is ready it serves as a base for discussions for the entire group of villagers. Various aspects of development can be discussed on this map such as the potential location for drinking water, tubewells, school buildings, latrines, etc. The resource map can also be useful in locating hazard points, locating the sick and disabled, or even families that need special attention and from where children can be chosen for sponsoring.

Transects

Purpose of the transects is to verify the field situation along with the community on site, verifying the community resource, its problems, and the potential opportunities. It is presented on a chart to facilitate interactive discussions on future course of action.

Method

Transects are of various types namely all round the settlement, of a specific resource, of a 'nullah' or a drainage, of a micro watershed, or along a village road. One begins by looking at the resource map of the village and marks out a path through it covering all the major resources enroute. The group of community members who are to accompany the outsiders on the transect are shown the route on the resource map and the transect exercise begins. While walking down on the transect, careful observations are made and questions asked to community members. Each area is observed for soil and land type, crop cultivation during different seasons, trees, animal husbandry, fisheries, problems and opportunities are prepared on the chart showing the profile area wise and discussed with larger group during the larger session.

Expected Output

The transect exercise helps produce a detailed inventory of the resources of the village matched with the specific problems encountered in each area type with an exploration of the potential opportunities for development. The underlying principle being that each problem is a potential opportunity for development.

Matrix Ranking

This exercise helps identify the reasons why the community makes certain choices by way of preferring one resource or type of resource as compared to another. It can be used to find out the preference of the community for crop varieties, types and breeds of livestock, trees, fodder, supplementary income generating activities, etc.

Method

After rapport building with the mixed group the item which is to be ranked is identified for example if it is matrix ranking of trees, then the different tree varieties are identified. It is preferable to ask the community 5-6 varieties of trees they all prefer. These are then represented in a linear fashion using the leaves or branches of the different species so that it is easy for every one to understand what is going on. Now, on the left side of the linear alignment are listed the various things for which trees are used by the community. This list is prepared by continuously asking the community 'what else?' till there are no more contributions to make. Now going down the list to each of the uses one ranks the selected 5-6 varieties, till the ranking is completed. Once all the options have been expanded upon, the community is asked to make a selection of only one variety if given a choice to choose only one. When this is done, they are asked to choose only from the remaining ones till the final ranking is done. Thus, it aims at locating the community's own criteria for choosing various things like trees or enterprise and ranking or scoring these according to their priorities.

Expected Output

The matrix ranking exercise helps us to understand the reasoning behind the choice of a specific variety and why it is important to consider the community's preference if one wants their participation in the programme.

Chappati Diagram

Chappati diagram or the Venn diagram exercise is conducted to identify which people or institutions are important to the community and what the level and frequency of their interaction is.

Method

A suitable spot is selected where sufficient people can assemble and the purpose of exercise is explained to the group. The group is asked to list the important institutions and the persons in the community and outside with whom they interact. Once the list is prepared, they are asked to select different sizes of circles (cut out of coloured papers) to represent each of them, selecting big circles for the important ones. Now taking a plain white paper and marking a dot in the centre of it, the group is asked to place each of the representative circle on this paper according to frequency of interaction and relationship. The ones that interact frequently and are closely related are placed closer to the centre, while the ones that interact less frequently are placed further away. Onlookers are asked if the circles (or chappatis) (chappati is a flat thin cake of unleavened bread, commonly eaten in northern India) are correctly placed. If they agree, then the location of the circle is made permanent by sticking it on to the sheet. When all the circles are placed, the correlation of the circles can be discussed:-

Expected Output

The 'Chappati' diagram can be used to understand the importance of different persons and institutions to the community and their interrelation. It can help identify which institutions can be strengthened and where intervention is required.

Wealth Ranking

This is a very interesting exercise that uses the community members' brain power to analyze the economic status of their peers. They have a natural curiosity to know everything possible about their fellow villagers, more so where economic status is concerned. Purchases, sales and amount of proceeds from any economic activity is usually a common community knowledge. The human brain is like a very efficient computer that is capable of analyzing each person's economic status considering various features about each person that they are familiar with like productive land holding size, house, agriculture practices, animals and other property. The use of this natural analytical power helps in overcoming the problem one normally faces in not being able to compare a person with less land that is productive with someone who has more land that is less productive.

Method

After initial rapport building with a small mixed group of persons familiar with the community, the purpose of the exercise is explained to them. They are first asked to name the heads of the households in the community and these are written on small pieces of papers. The group is now asked to describe how many types of wealth groups exist in the community. Their answers generally begin with some vague answers like, everyone here is poor, but with proper facilitation they usually come up with 3-4 groups like rich, medium, poor and very poor. The group is now asked to describe each of these groups by way of profiling them; and they do so in a most interesting way allocating the groups on the basis of extent of agriculture, sowing capacity, family size, other property, use of motorized vehicle, use of luxury items, etc. When the wealth groups are established, they are handed over the slips on which the names of heads of the households were written and asked to classify these. In a short period of time, all the slips of paper are quickly classified. Further classification within each group can be made to get it in serial order.

Expected Output

This exercise helps in identifying the poorest of the poor in a community to thus identify those who are in need of help first. It can be from such homes that the children for sponsoring can be selected.

Casual Diagrams

Casual or Impact diagrams are useful to find out the inter-links between events and trace the cumulative result. It can also be used for working backwards and finding out cause of the problem.

Method

After initial rapport building the group is asked to identify the most important problem they are facing. This might be one single thing or a series of problems. The causal diagram can then be carried out for each of the problems. The identified problem is represented in the centre of a clear place using a diagram or an object which every one can identify easily. Now tracing backwards the group is asked to identify the various causes of this problem and each of these is either written or represented by a diagram. Further, the individual causes are also traced backwards to find out what resulted in them, using arrows to show which one resulted in what. The causal diagram soon emerges as a maze of circles and arrows. When completed, it is easy to identify the major reasons and use the diagram to involve the community in discussing ways to overcome the problem.

Expected Output

Major problems with the various causative agents can be identified for discussion and the community can be involved in exploring the options to overcome the problems.

A corollary of the causal diagram is the 'Impact Diagram' which can be used to find out 'The Result of a Programme', the intervention or even a problem.

Profile of Women's Work Day

This exercise is carried out to find out women's role in the community and appreciate the long hours of work that are her portion of the daily routine. Knowing this is essential to locate a suitable time for meetings, or training programme or even starting a new programme.

Method

This exercise is done mainly with a group of women and often the presence of a man from among the community can be a hindrance. After rapport building an average day in their lives, starting with the time of getting up and so on till they go to sleep at night, the various activities are either drawn or represented using different representative articles so that everyone can understand.

Expected Output

This exercise after completion can often help identify the negative effects that outside intervention programmes have had on women. It can also help in identifying activities of drudgery that women have to put up with, which once they are freed from, they can play a more constructive and positive role in the community.

One Page Story

The one page story is like an executive summary of all the exercises conducted in the community with various aspects picked out to give a summary of the community, its background, its problems, survival strategy and potential opportunities.

Method

The one page story should be prepared by the different groups of participants who carried out the various PLA exercises. After each group has made its presentation and everyone has made their own observations and noted them, the groups break off to prepare the 'one-page story'. The one page story should fulfil the following criteria:

- It should not exceed one page
- It should have only three paragraphs

The first paragraph should have details of the history of the community, how it came into being, where it is located, and a mention of major crisis that it has experienced till the present.

The second paragraph should consist of a C/V analysis, or a listing of the major capacities/capabilities (C) and the vulnerabilities (V) that the community possesses. These should be clearly listed so that one can get a clear idea on which vulnerabilities have to be overcome and which capabilities of the community constitute its survival strategy.

The third paragraph should consist of solutions suggested by the community for overcoming its vulnerabilities. This would normally come out more conclusively in the final exercise called the village/community development plan.

The one-page stories prepared by each group are read out by them and the best and most concise presentation is selected. The first two paragraphs of this story are then presented to the community before the concluding exercise and they are asked to add, correct or modify as the case may be.

Expected Output

The exercise helps prepare a summary of the findings about the community based on all the exercises conducted.

Village/Community Resource Development Plan

The purpose of this exercise is to review all the information gathered from the community and after understanding from this what the survival strategy is, to prepare with the community a village/community resource development plan.

Method

After the sequence of the basic exercises has been carried out, the community as well as the outsiders who have been facilitating PLA exercises gather together at a central place in the village. Ideally this is also the place where the village resource map was drawn. Each group of the community which was involved in the preparation of outputs of various exercises are asked to make a presentation of the information collected and final triangulation is carried out. As each presentation is made the remaining members of the community are asked to identify the capacities and capabilities (the positive strengths that the community has) and the vulnerabilities (the areas of weakness that need to be overcome). This is known as C/V analysis. The C/V analysis consists of listing in priority the capacities (placing the greatest strength on the top) and the vulnerabilities placing the greatest weakness at the bottom.

The community is then encouraged to plan a development programme building on its capacities to overcome the vulnerabilities. These are listed in the form of a plan of action. After this rough list is prepared, it is sorted out in the following sequence:

1.	No Cost	No Technology
2.	Low Cost	Indigenous Technology
3.	Medium Cost	Medium Technology
4.	High Cost	Hi-tech

Care is taken to ensure that activities identified are those that will benefit on a priority the poorest of the poor and also fairly a large section of the community. This can be ensured by carrying out this exercise in the area where the largest number of marginalized people live. The facilitators have to be sensitive to the voicing of selfish single person benefiting suggestions by cross checking with the larger group if that activity will in fact benefit a large section of the community. When this is done effectively, several vested interests get curtailed.

After the plan of action is completed, each aspect of it is re-discussed and specific activities to achieve it are, listed. For each activity, responsibility is fixed in consultation with the community and by when it has to be done. An evaluation team consisting mainly of the community is selected by the community to review progress against plan of action at periodic intervals.

Costs and budgets are also worked out for various activities with the community actively participating and when one does this one usually finds costs working out to be much less than when planning otherwise.

Expected Outcome

If PLA exercises are conducted in the community with active participation of the people, it usually leads to the framing of a very effective plan of action. In exceptional cases when outsiders are not able to stay within the community or when community members are not available all through the time of the interaction because of other priorities, and there is not enough spontaneity to generate the village resource development plan; at such times it is advisable to identify the different issues that came up during the various exercises, particularly the transect, livelihood analysis, seasonality diagram and impact diagram and rank these according to priority.

Conflict Analysis

This exercise is conducted in situations where it is found that there are conflicts in the community and where it is desirable to find out what the causes of these are.

Method

It is better to conduct this exercise on the second or third day after interaction has begun with the community and when they feel a little more free to share information that might be sensitive. Using the same technique as with pie diagram they are asked to list all the causes of the conflict in the village. After these have been enumerated, they are asked to imagine that all the conflicts that take place in the village are equal to one rupee=100 paise. They are now asked to mark out chunks to represent how many paise would represent the part played by different causes.

Expected Outcome

Once the various causes of the conflict have been identified and also the extent to which they play a part, the group is asked what they do in the event of a conflict and who they go to for resolving the problem. The information can be useful in sensitizing outsiders to the emotional climate and sensitivity of the community.

Water Resources and Use Pattern

The object is to find out what are the various water resources available to the community and also how they use it for various purposes.

Method

Using the same techniques as for pie diagram, one finds out from the group the various water sources from where the community gets its water, these may be from the river, lake, ponds, wells, etc., depending on access. The pie diagram thus shows what the percentage source according to use is. A similar pie diagram is now prepared to find out average individual household water use pattern in terms of which water is used for domestic work like cooking, washing clothes, bathing, drinking, washing animals, irrigating, etc. Several different pie diagrams can be used to find out on the basis of source and also on the basis of use.

Expected Outcome

Besides giving a lot of information on water access and water use patterns it helps understand why specific type of water is used for specific purposes. For example, outsiders often presume when they see borewells that the community has access to it and is using it for drinking when in fact they might not be. Several options can thus be explored for overcoming specific problems that exist.

Commercial Activity in the Community

It is extension of livelihood analysis by listing the various commercial activities and fitting them on to a seasonality calendar to find out in which season which activity gains predominance. One usually finds that rural communities depend on multiple activities as sources of income. They usually do not span the same way throughout the year because of their link with availability and surpluses in different seasons.

Method

As mentioned above, the exercise is a combination of the livelihood analysis and seasonality exercises. Another way is to examine each surplus and do an impact diagram of how the surplus is taken care of for marketing, consumption and storage.

Expected Outcome

The outcome of these exercises is a clearer understanding of the commercial activity in existence in the community, its scope and limitations. It leads to an understanding of the bottlenecks that exist specially with local market demand and seasonal surpluses.

Cattle Diseases and Local Treatment Techniques

This exercise is conducted to find out what are the common diseases affecting cattle, what name the local people give it, what they recognize as symptoms of the disease and what indigenous methods they have for its treatment. The exercise is particularly useful where one sees a lot of animal husbandry activity.

Method

The exercise can be used not only to find out about cattle diseases but also but also about human diseases. The various locally recognized diseases are enumerated and called by local name as the community calls it. The symptoms of each disease are discussed with the community and these are then written down. The community is now asked what they do when the disease occurs, the treatment they give etc. The community is asked about the efficacy of this local treatment and asked to identify diseases for which they have no treatment of their own.

Expected Outcome

This exercise helps us appreciate the community's knowledge about the animals being reared by them. It also helps us to get a clear understanding of the crisis they face when any disease is beyond their capacity to handle. On the basis of symptoms mentioned it is easy for an experienced veterinarian to identify the disease and recommend a solution which local active youth can be trained to do. This way very specific area wise need-based training can be given to interested persons to act as barefoot veterinarians.

Do's of PLA

1. Do enlist the support of the insider – school teachers, village leaders, etc. – till confident that you can manage without them.
2. Fix appointments with the participants/key informants on the eve of an interview/exercise.
3. Recognize and respect the villagers and their knowledge. Make them feel that what they know is important. Old people are the most experienced and knowledgeable. Try sincerely to be a learner for a few days.
4. Be alert and sensitive to the mood of the village and the villagers. If they are preoccupied and busy with market day or sowing or getting in their harvest before it rains, the last thing they would want is to sit and spend 3 or 4 hours of precious time talking to outsiders.
5. Join in village tasks. This helps to bring a sense of equality. Think of other ways of bringing this about.
6. Do make the sessions enjoyable for the villagers, for you and for other participants. If they are boring, well then...

Dont's of PLA

1. You guessed it right. Don't lecture! and don't interrupt!
2. Don't put your agenda before theirs.
3. Don't move around the village as if you owned it.
4. Don't be put off by any non-participation beyond your control. Try to think what is going wrong. Talk to other villagers and ask their advice on what to do and how to go about it. Don't hesitate to ask villagers for advice.
5. Don't allow a we-they situation to evolve. Consciously keep mixing with the villagers specially during the evening group presentations, look around and see where your outsider colleagues are positioned, are they interspersed with the villagers or they are in a group by themselves.
6. Don't stick with only one section of the population either and exclude others – unless for a specific purpose.
7. Don't exclude women and children.

PLA is therefore effective because it seeks to understand the survival strategy of the community, appraise it and show ways to enhance the capability of that effort to ensure sustainability. The new paradigm of PLA proposes a shift from the paternalistic approach of "I tell you what you ought to do" to a more realistic partnership. Early efforts of PLA have to facilitate a concentration of their vast information to focus on what they have done to 'survive'. When this has been adequately done by the initial rounds of exercises, relevant information of the capacities and vulnerabilities of the community becomes adequately available. The community and outsiders are now in a position to discuss as equal partners what possible solutions are and what possibilities exist for redirecting inside effort and also for outside intervention. This is the point at which the village resource development plan is made and responsibilities fixed. The community members are the best managers of scarce resources. With PLA, the community's role consistently increases. When this is done sensitively there is no conflict with goal ownership, and therefore sustainability is spontaneous.

Because of its strong facilitative role and the widespread participation that it ensures, PLA can often unleash and often liberate long suppressed dreams of the community. Enthusiasm can be very great and therefore will need steady support and interaction to keep it productively utilized. Thus, PLA is a dynamic process and the dynamics of interacting with the community in a new mode can often result in the generation of a lot of very interesting information which is fascinating. Much of PLA success depends on willingness of practitioners to share the information that they gathered freely. This must continue for the process to continue to be innovative and dynamic. The inventiveness and flexibility also should be maintained. Hence PLA has the ability to change lives and attitudes.

References

"Guidelines for Watershed Development", (Revised–2001) Government of India, Ministry of Rural Development, Department of Land Resources, 2001.

Jayakaran, Ravi I., *Participatory Learning and Action*, User Guide and Manual, World Vision of India, 1996.

"Participatory Planning of Watershed Programme, Part II", Institute of Rural Management, Jaipur, 1997.

Training Courses on Soil Conservation and Watershed Management (1994), Directorate of Soil Conservation and Watershed Management (NWDPRA) Department of Agriculture, Government of Rajasthan, Jaipur.

"Watershed Development", Proceedings of Danida's International Workshop on Watershed Development held at Hubli and Bangalore, Jenson, J.R.(ed.), T. Sawhney, S.L. Seth and P.Kumar, *WDCU Publication No.1*, 1995.

"Watershed Development in Rajasthan: Activities and Achievements", Watershed Development and Soil Conservation Department, Rajasthan, 2002.

8

Community Management of Lift Irrigation Projects

In 1978, the Government of India took special steps for development of rural areas of the country by constituting district rural development agencies through which programmes for poverty alleviation were to be implemented. 'Tribal Sub-Plan' was also started for tribal areas. Due to geographical character of the area, there are many rivers, rivulets, deep nallas in which water flows abundantly during rainy season but could not be utilized for irrigating agricultural fields. Besides big irrigation projects, there is vast scope for anicuts, lift irrigation projects, development of tanks, etc. Rainwater harvesting structures are being constructed by the rural community for conservation of water during rains and make use of it for irrigation of crops as and when there is need for irrigation. But there are sites in river basins or back waters of irrigation dams where rain water collects in large quantities. Cultivators lift water from such storage tanks/nallas through electric motors, carry it through canals and distributaries to their fields. If need be, storage tanks are also constructed on way to fields.

Minor irrigation schemes consist of the following:

1. Lift irrigation schemes.
2. Anicuts/tanks.

3. Community diesel pumps.
4. Private irrigation wells under Jeevan Dhara scheme.
5. Deepening of private wells through free blasting by groundwater department.
6. Soil conservation and water conservation programme.

A field study was made regarding execution and working of lift irrigation projects in tribal areas of Rajasthan. Experience of community participation was also analyzed. It was found as under:

Anicuts were constructed. Scheme of construction of anicuts is really useful in areas where sub-soil water level is deteriorating day by day. It is a productive scheme, 100 per cent financed by government but no contribution of any sort from people either in cash or labour was made.

Soil conservation works were carried out in private fields where 10 per cent people's participation is compulsory. Earthen check dams could also be constructed in common lands where required peóple's participation from SC/ST is only 5 per cent. Thus, 90 per cent to 95 per cent expenditure of soil conservation works is borne by the government. There were 20 lift irrigation schemes executed in the study area. Out of them, world bank assisted 6, whereas 14 were financed through tribal sub-plan budget. People's participation of tribals is 10 per cent.

To provide irrigation facilities to small and marginal SC/ST cultivators, the Government of India started Million Wells Scheme known by the name of 'Jeevan Dhara' to increase productivity of their lands.

Diesel pumpset of 5 HP was provided free of cost along with 25 feet suction pipe and 25 feet delivery pipe of rubber. Maintenance of pumpset is responsibility of group members. Five HP pumpset costing around Rs.18,000 is sanctioned to individual small and marginal tribal farmers provided they have a source of irrigation. A 50 per cent subsidy and 50 per cent bank loan is provided. PVC pipe measuring 100 metre is supplied to small and marginal tribal farmers on 50 per cent cost.

For sustainable development, it is essential that the benefit of schemes should continue uninterruptedly in the long run also. Hence, unless people's direct involvement is there at planning and execution stage, maintenance at future date after initial commencement of the project will continue to be a headache. Moreover, lakhs of amount spent to complete the project go waste if benefits cease to continue to poor beneficiaries. Hence, the people's participation and its importance in rural development programmes.

R.P. Joshi of MDS University of Ajmer (Rajasthan) conducted a research study of execution of lift irrigation schemes in tribal district of Rajasthan. Findings of the study are summarized below:

Lift Irrigation Projects in Tribal District Banswara

Lift irrigation schemes were executed in district Banswara as under:

Panchayat Samiti	*World Bank Fund*	*TAD & other Fund*	*Total*
Anand Puri	6	14	20
Talwara	4	25	29
Sajjan Garh	11	9	20
Pipal Khoot	10	27	37
Kushal Garh	5	6	11
Ghatol	4	12	16
Gadhi	13	9	22
Bagidora	4	11	15
Total	57	113	70

Due to geographical advantage, there is huge scope for lift irrigation in hilly or tribal regions which are also generally located in hilly areas. During the last decade, 170 such schemes were implemented in Banswara district alone either through world bank assisted scheme or Tribal Area Development

(TAD) programme executed through special central assistance. Average cost was Rs. 6-7 lakhs. Area covered under irrigation per scheme was 35-40 hectares on an average. Average cost per hectare comes to around Rs. 25,000 to Rs. 30,000. Main conditions for taking up lift scheme are:

1. Minimum number of 10 cultivators should form a group for lift scheme.
2. Minimum area required is 130 bighas cultivated land. It could be at the most 250 bighas.
3. People should be ready to contribute 20 per cent in cash or labour. About 80 per cent funds are provided through the World Bank.
4. Additional assistance of 10 per cent is also given from TAD budget provided 70 per cent farmers within the group are tribals.
5. People's contribution is around Rs. 25,000, out of which Rs.10,000 should be deposited in bank account of the committee and balance in kind/labour.
6. Water can be lifted from back waters of Mahi or Kadana irrigation project or perennial nalla where water remains available at least up to April month of the year.

Such proposals duly signed by all the cultivators are submitted to DRDA along with revenue record and map of the area. DRDA officials call a public meeting in the village, explain the working details of the scheme and get an executive committee formed for implementing the project. Chairman and secretary open a bank account with minimum public contribution of Rs.10,000. It is on such basis that sanction is issued by DRDA after proper survey. Cost of survey is approx. Rs. 100 per hectare.

Steps for execution of lift can be summarized as under:

- Request by cultivators along with a list of members and a map.
- Deposit of Rs. 10,000 in a bank as public contribution.

- Meeting of members to form a committee and elect chairman and secretary.
- Excavation of civil work, construction of motor room, distribution tank, field outlet tank and platform.
- Supply of motors and pumpsets by the state government of approximately 70 per cent project cost.
- Deposit cost of electric line and transformer of 30-60 HP as per RSEB demand notice. It is approximately 15 per cent of the cost of the project ranging from Rs. 1 lahk to Rs. 1.5 lakh.
- Power connection.
- Installation and handing over the schemes to the committee for operation and maintenance.

Jeevan Dhara Wells

In panchayats where neither Mahi waters irrigate nor there are lift irrigation schemes, irrigation is done through dug wells. To provide irrigation facilities to small and marginal SC/ST cultivators, the Government of India started Million Wells Scheme known by the name of 'Jeevan Dhara' to increase productivity of their lands. An amount up to Rs. 35,000 is sanctioned, payable in three instalments to SC/ST farmers who do not have irrigation facilities. Farmers themselves dig the wells. Standard depth is 18 metres and width 4 metres. Up to 40 per cent expenditure can be done on material component and 60 per cent on labour.

Deepening of Wells by Blasting/Boring

Those SC/ST farmers, who have already got a well/source of irrigation but have not been benefited under Jeevan Dhara scheme, provision exists for providing them assistance for deepening of existing well.

- Deepening through blasting Rs. 9,000.
- Deepening through boring Rs. 10,000.

In non-command areas, where private irrigation wells exist but groundwater level has gone so low that well becomes dry or water exhausts away, assistance is given to such marginal and small SC/ST farmers. Facilities are provided to farmers on application made to Vikas Adhikari of Panchayat Samiti. Sanction along with Rs. 9,000 each is sent to Rajasthan Groundwater Department (RGWD). RGWD blasts 72 holes in six rounds through blasting machines. Debris is to be cleaned by beneficiary cultivators at their own expenses. Normally 300 cultivators are benefited each year in the district. Anandpuri Panchayat Samiti gets a share of about 50 Jeevan Dhara wells every year.

On a similar pattern if boring is required, it is also done through boring machine of RGWD. Sanctioned amount along with the list of beneficiaries is sent to RGWD by DRDA. Details of boring of wells of beneficiaries could not be made available because due to hard rock in Anandpuri Panchayat Samiti, cultivators preferred blasting rather than deepening through boring in wells.

Community Pumpsets

To give irrigation facility to marginal and small ST farmers, this scheme was launched. Terms and conditions were as under:

- Minimum land area should be 18 bighas in one block.
- Group should consist of 3-5 small or marginal farmers.
- They should own a well or a water source of river/nalla/tank/anicut nearer the land to be irrigated.
- Diesel pumpset of 5 HP is provided free of cost along with 25 feet suction pipe and 25 feet delivery pipe of rubber. Total cost is around Rs.18,000.
- If depth of nalla is more, remaining pipe is procured by member cultivators themselves.

Diesel pumpset is supplied by Rajasthan Agro-Industries Corporation (RAIC). Project officer, TAD arranges the supply of pumpsets from RAIC to Panchayat Samiti which distributes pumpsets to beneficiaries groups. About 15-20 groups are benefited every year. Maintenance of pumpset is responsibility of group members. There is also a chairman and secretary of the group.

There were 93 persons intimately and directly connected with the lift irrigation programme who were interviewed by research assistant and investigator personally. Results of such responses have been analyzed in depth.

- 71 per cent cultivators beneficiaries were small and marginal farmers. Average income before irrigation facilities was not more than Rs. 2,000 per hectare.
- Maximum benefit was derived by big farmers whose irrigated area increased by 755 per cent as against small and marginal farmers whose area increase was 300 per cent and 250 per cent respectively, though all the farmers were tribals.
- Prior to scheme, no area was fully irrigated. It was either unirrigated or partly irrigated whereas after execution of lift irrigation schemes, 100 per cent area was fully irrigated.
- Prior to scheme, *rabi* crop was of only gram and mustard which also was produced due to moisture retained in the soil. After the scheme, whole of the area is directly irrigated through lift water, well water or nallah/river waters.
- Farmers continued to grow cereal crops of wheat and barley only which were necessary either for their domestic consumption or sale in markets. No efforts were made to change the pattern to commercial crops like mustard, cotton, sugarcane, etc., which suited the soil and was also in demand.
- The analysis of survey shows that only 6 per cent cultivators gained the benefit of crops. It also indicates indifferent attitude of farmers towards raising their income and standard of living through optimum utilization of irrigation facility.

- General cooperation of government officials was there. There was no beneficiary who complained about non-cooperation of officials. However, 87 per cent appreciated it but 13 per cent felt that it was normal cooperation. All non-officials responded favourably and opined that cooperation of DRDA and Panchayat Samiti officials was very good in implementation of the programmes.
- Cultivators of course complained about indifferent attitude of agricultural supervisors and officers of agricultural department. Attitude of officials of RSEB was also apathetic.
- As regards community participation, the analysis of this study revealed that cultivator beneficiaries became ready to contribute their 10 per cent share only after 10 to 15 extension meetings. Though community was enthusiastic in the beginning but it could not own the scheme. They continued to treat it as government scheme and found faults with it rather than running it successfully to their advantage.
- Some of the members defaulted in payment of their share of electricity dues or digging their canals or fixing outlet pipes. Default of few members resulted in whole community to suffer due to non-cooperation in the scheme.

Implementation of Lift Irrigation Schemes

Perception of Beneficiaries

Beneficiaries were well aware of the need for irrigation and they were eager to get the benefits but with minimum or no public contribution. Individual selfishness is more dominant than community feeling. They think that it is responsibility of the government, to do everything for them. Hence, beneficiaries were critical about the implementation of the scheme and tried to find fault in every respect as under:

- *Poor Quality of PVC Pipes*: Due to pressure of water there is breakage in PVC pipes. There is no provision for renewal or replacement. Hence, they suggested to procure PVC pipes of 6 kg pressure, Kissan Brand or in which supplier gives guarantee of replacement at least for 1-2 years. Alternatively, farmers should also be involved in purchase of pipes and spares through purchase committee.
- *Non-supply of Spares*: There is no provision for supply of replace-valves, bends, starters, volt metre capacitators, ampere metres and branch-line pipes. Beneficiaries faced problems for want of such spares in running and maintenance of lift irrigation schemes after once commissioning them. Government should get few spares at least for six months or one year at the time of initial purchase of motor, etc.
- *Lack of Technical Guidance*: DRDA officials did not give any technical training to the members for running and proper maintenance of electric motors in the beginning. Government officials neglected the scheme after initial commissioning of lift irrigation projects. In future, DRDA must arrange such training through technical people of RSEB as part of the project programme.
- *Problem of Voltage Fluctuation*: Instead of 440 voltage, actual voltages 280-300 are fluctuating. It results in frequent burning of motors resulting in economic loss to the community and stoppage of benefits till motors are replaced.
- *Irregular Power Supply*: Power supply is not available many times when irrigation is badly needed for crops. Crops dry due to lack of irrigation in case of power failure. Transmitter of high power should be installed on grid station concerned to prevent such problems.

- *Exorbitant Billing on Flat-rate Basis*: Cultivators use motors for irrigation purpose only for four months but billing is done on a flat-rate basis for all the 12 months. Meter readers do not record the actual reading but mark 'D' (defective motor) or 'L' (lock) and send exorbitant bills. Electric connection of Dokar I lift irrigation was disconnected due to non-payment of exorbitant bill of Rs. 43,000. On an average yearly bill is around Rs. 14,000.
- *Indifferent Attitude of RSEB Officials*: In case of complaint about exorbitant billing, RSEB engineers take away the metre and start charging on flat rate basis which causes the same problem of heavy billing and consequent non-payment by farmers. Hence, it is suggested that charges should be recovered on the basis of metre reading which is possible only when electric metres are installed in all projects.
- *Non-payment of Dues by Members*: Some irresponsible members do not cooperate in sharing the electricity bills or pay for maintenance charges for replacements of motors or pipes. This results in failure of the whole project.
- *Lack of Special Production Programme in the Area*: Agricultural department or animal husbandry department have not taken up any intensive programme for propagation of commercial crops or improvement of cattle breed. Due to production of traditional cereal crops, desired rise in incomes has not been possible.
- *Limited Horticulture Development Programme:* Only 10 tribal cultivators in each Panchayat Samiti are supplied fruit plants every year. Such programme could have been taken on a very large scale in view of the potential of the area specially for the mangoes, which have been cultivated traditionally.

Perception of Officials

The government officials perception was generally regarding non-cooperation of the community and lack of enthusiasm as under:

- *Government Dependence*: Officials complain that community is highly dependent on government support. After commissioning of the project, they still expect the government to run the scheme and supply all spares from time to time. Community should own the scheme and bear the running and maintenance cost.
- *Non-payment*: Officials visualize failure of running the scheme on account of refusal of some members to pay their share. In most of the cases, non-payment of electricity bills has resulted in stoppage of the scheme and the whole investment has gone waste.
- *Lack of Enthusiasm for New Crops Among Tribals*: Officials feel that tribals are uneducated or illiterate. They do not understand the implication of latest technology or application of pesticides for prevention of white ant. Moreover, difficulty of marketing for cotton or sugarcane also come in the way.
- *Lack of Interest or Enthusiasm Among Tribals*: Tribals are more interested in fairs and festivals, dancing and drinking. They do not take real interest in raising productivity or farm income. They are contented people and lack enthusiasm for improved agricultural practices, orchards or commercial crops.
- *Lack of Finances*: Poverty is at the back of traditional cultivation, sowing of cereal crops only, non-use of improved seeds, pesticides or chemical fertilizers. Hence, not much can be done in spite of increased irrigation facility through lift irrigation schemes.

Perception of Non-officials

Non-officials also share the views of beneficiaries except that they find fault with member cultivators regarding non-payment of maintenance charges and electricity bills. They also feel that enthusiasm shown by the farmers at initial stage does not subsist long due to inter-member disputes due to shortage of power supply for irrigation of crops.

They suggested that irresponsible members should not be included in the project to avoid disconnection for non-payment. Cultivators should not let loose their cattle so as to damage the Zaid crop raised by few farmers. Proper technical guidance should be continued as follow up by RSEB and DRDA officials for successful running of the schemes after initial commissioning. Example of Vanda I, Vanda II and Vanda III was quoted as an ideal example where lift irrigation projects have been successfully running due to full cooperation of members. As against this, Dokar I project has been closed for the last two years for non-payment of electricity bills. Roniya project successfully ran for two years but power connection is disconnected due to non-payment of electricity bills.

Jeevan Dhara Wells

Perception of Beneficiaries

Beneficiaries think that the scheme is really useful for the needy. But, there is hard rock right from surface. Groundwater level is very deep. Blasting machine does not reach as per scheduled programme. Cultivators face financial problem in cleaning the blasted rock or de-watering of wells.

Perception of Officials

Officials feel that sincere cultivators complete the work but insincere cultivators misuse the money for marriage or drinking. They are interested in benefit only but not in sharing responsibility. People's cooperation in cleaning the blasted rocks is not readily available. Groundwater officials become desperate when blasting machine reaches the site but find that blasted rock is still lying in the well and has not been cleaned. It is not ready by scheduled time as intimated to the cultivators. It is really indifferent attitude of cultivators as well as lack of synchronization which is responsible for incomplete Jeevan Dhara wells.

Perception of Non-officials

Even non-officials agreed that Jeevan Dhara wells remained incomplete where farmers wanted to misuse money. Sincere people completed the wells and got the benefit of the scheme. It is really a beneficial and productive scheme for the poor and needy cultivators.

Group Diesel Pumpsets

Perception of Beneficiaries

Beneficiaries highly appreciated the scheme. Since facility of irrigation wells is not available with many cultivators, and there is hard rock for digging new well, it is very casy to lift water from perennial flowing nallas through diesel pumpset in nearby farmers' fields as per requirements of crops. However, the person responsible for maintenance complained regarding non-payment of maintenance dues by other group members. Mutual disputes arise on sharing of the use of diesel pumpset or non-payment of cost of maintenance. It is advisable to take 10 per cent contribution from members for proper upkeep and maintenance of diesel pumpset for future use.

Perception of Officials

Officials feel that due to many perennial nallas, the demand for diesel pumpset is very high. Till 1993, there were complaints of re-sale of diesel pumpset also by tribal farmers. But thereafter farmers have realized its use. There have been no complaints of re-sale for the last five to six years. The scheme is really beneficial but problem of maintenance is there due to absence of mechanics in the village or difficulty of sharing cost of repair by members of the group. One who gets it repaired, treats it as his individually owned diesel pumpset. This causes conflict mutually. But, on the whole, it is a beneficial and successful scheme.

Perception of Non-officials

Since the demand is much more as compared to the target, people's representatives feel that selection of beneficiaries should be at the level of PRIs. Superior officers should also physically inspect on site as a follow up for guidance. They also felt the responsibility for maintenance is not being satisfactorily performed by their group members.

Anicuts

Perception of Beneficiaries

Villagers appreciated the scheme of anicuts which were utilized for storage of water and lifting it for irrigation. Dhanku and Kahavada village anicuts had proved a boon because these anicuts were being used for lift irrigation projects. After silting also, new land is created in nallas for future cultivation. In case of de-silting, fertile soil is transferred to cultivated fields so as to increase the productivity of soil which is not deep enough due to sloping and hilly lands.

Perception of Officials

The officials favoured anicuts where they are really beneficial either for lift irrigation or raising the sub-soil water. In case there is a very small nalla where enough water does not flow, it is wasteful since it does not meet the cost-benefit ratio. Hence, anicuts should be constructed after verifying technical feasibility and not on the basis of political will without proper justification.

Perception of Non-officials

The non-officials favoured the anicuts and supported it fully because it met the local needs of the villagers, stored water, raised sub-soil water, facilitated lift irrigation and even after silting, land was created for cultivation by collection of productive soil content in the nallah. The scheme is very popular with people's representatives though complaints of misuse of money by PRIs officials or lack of technical support do exist here or there. Employment was also generated because tribals were poor and needy and most of the anicuts were constructed under employment assurance scheme. Each anicuts cost from Rs. 50,000 to Rs. 5 lakh and provided sufficient employment to local tribals.

Thus, looking to hilly terrain of Anandpuri block and high potential of lift irrigation schemes due to availability of Mahi and Anas rivers as well as back waters of Kadana project, minor irrigation schemes have a very good scope in the area. The programme is beneficial, productive and of direct use to productivity and income of tribal farmers. Successful implementation of minor irrigation schemes can change the fate of tribals. Additional income can be generated. Debt incidence of Mahajan can be reduced. Agriculture may not remain a gamble in rains. Government officials should of course give proper technical backup, some technical training, follow up after initial commissioning, on the spot physical verification as per prescribed norms and re-start the failed projects by holding community meetings with the help of local leaders and Panchayati Raj Institutions. On the whole, the programme is very successful provided loopholes here and there are properly plugged to make it more effective.

Suggestions

Looking to hilly terrain and high potential of lift irrigation schemes due to availability of Mahi and Anas rivers as well as back waters of Kadana project, minor irrigation schemes have a very good scope in the area. The programme is beneficial, productive and of direct use to productivity and income of tribal farmers. Successful implementation of minor irrigation schemes can change the fate of tribals. Additional income can be generated. Debt incidence of Mahajan can be reduced. Agriculture may not remain a gamble in rains.

Technical Support by Government Agencies

Government officials should give proper technical back-up, some technical training, follow up after initial commissioning, on the spot physical verification as per prescribed norms and re-start the failed projects by holding community meetings with the help of local leaders and PRIs.

Support of Agricultural Department

Agriculture extension agencies should have intensive programme for propagating commercial crops as well as their marketing through Krishi Upaj Mandi.

Horticulture Development

Looking to the terrain and climate, horticulture development programme should also be intensified.

Sympathetic Attitude of Electricity Board

RSEB should arrange training of tribal cultivators regarding maintenance of motors and running of scheme successfully. Charges as per actual metre reading should be recovered instead of flat rate. Transformers should be installed at proper places to ensure regular voltage.

Role of Panchayati Raj Institutions

It was revealed during the survey that DRDA approached the cultivators, organized their meetings and formed their executive committee. Gram Sabha should be organized by the Panchayat to discuss utility and implementation of minor irrigation programmes which are of direct benefit to them. In such meetings, government officials should only explain the terms and conditions of the schemes. PRIs should be responsible for people's participation and maintenance of the lift schemes. It should be responsibility of the panchayat to select Jeevan Dhara beneficiaries and ensure that the wells are completed. Direct sanction by DRDA without involvement of PRIs creates problems regarding people's participation to the required extent.

Role of Voluntary Agencies

Tribals are poor and needy and lack latest knowledge and awareness. Voluntary agencies can organize tribals to take benefit of schemes by creating awareness among them and ensuring share of people's participation in running the schemes.

Thus, it is clear from the analysis of the constraints identified in successful implementation of minor irrigation that active involvement and participation of the tribals is yet to take a concrete shape to form a movement. This calls for evolving a definite multi-pronged strategy which may encompass awareness generation, resource mobilization and sustainable interest and enthusiasm as its key components. Needless to say that PRIs alone are capable of taking care of this strategy and ensuring its proper follow-up in the field. They can rely upon necessary support of official and voluntary agencies in their mission for rural development and upon people by imparting and cultivating a proper outlook among the beneficiaries, namely, tribals who are still illiterate, poor and backward. It will be with a missionary mission alone that dream of Bapu's Gram Swarajya can be realized.

PRIs were constituted basically with the purpose of associating people's representatives in planning at the base level as well as ensuring community participation in execution of rural development works and their maintenance afterwards. But people generally treated development works as government works and not village works owned by them. Community development programme could become development programme for the people but it could never become development programme of the people. It has been realized that people's participation has been lacking to the desired extent while implementing rural development programmes. Efforts were made to involve people by way of 'public contribution' in 1952 and by way of 'Panchayati Raj' in 1959 but active involvement of the community could not be achieved. People's elected representatives, of course, participated in planning, execution and monitoring of rural development programmes but they could not convert them into people's programmes. People around political leaders could snatch away such benefits. Really, the poor is still cornered and helpless.

Reference

Joshi, R.P., People's Participation in Lift Irrigation Projects in Tribal Areas of Rajasthan, 1999.

9

Community Management of Groundwater Resources

Surface water has been managed by community through tank irrigation in the states of Karnataka and Andhra Pradesh since times immemorial but groundwater management through community is of recent origin. Of late, individual wells or tubewells were being used for irrigation of agriculture. With the increased need for drinking water, state tubewells were drilled for meeting the requirement of drinking water in urban as well as rural areas. The programme of community tubewells started on a large scale in Uttar Pradesh in 1950-51 when 200 tubewells were constructed. Uttar Pradesh Public Tubewells Project was launched in 1980.

Public Tubewells

The World Bank-aided public tubewells (PTWs) were designed with superior technology. Field water distributaries and feeders were dug. Electricity was assured for 16-18 hours. Agricultural extension service was also dovetailed with it. Farmers were involved in water distribution systems. PTWs are meant to benefit the marginal and poorer farmers. Tubewells are in clusters of 25 each in areas where economically backward people reside and are engaged in farming. There were 559 tubewells installed in phase I (1980-83) and another 24,000 in phase II (1983-87). The pattern of water distribution reflects the extent of farmers' participation in management of water resources from PTWs. Provision for farmers' participation was made at the layout stage itself. Benefits were quite gratifying. Compared to the base year, the yield of paddy and wheat increased by 53 per cent and 40 per cent respectively. Cropping intensity increased by 34 per cent and the number of farmers using improved seeds increased from 76 per cent to 93 per cent.

Management System

Submersible pumps are fitted by the state and are operated on electricity. Water is pumped into the distribution chamber which is an elevated tank. From the tank, water flows in two directions through underground PVC pipes up to outlet valves called *kundis*. There is no transmission loss up to *kundis*, since water flows under ground. Each tubewell has a part-time operator who opens *kundi* gates. Majority of tubewells have a command of 100 hectares and serves 150-200 beneficiaries. Maintenance up to *kundis* is taken care of by the irrigation department.

Community Participation

Returns on investment are determined by water accessibility and its utilization. Farmer is to develop accessibility to water. The moment he develops an access, he has to decide how to get optimum utilization. The extent of accessibility and pattern of utilization reflects farmer's participation in irrigation management. The responsibility of tubewells, management rests divided equally between farmers and officials of irrigation and agricultural departments. Farmers through two committees – DAC and TAMC – would manage the irrigation system. Water is distributed through open earthen channels after flow from *kundis*. Channels were constructed by the state as a part of the project but maintained by farmers. A *kundi* serves a specified number of farmers on each day. The operation of water distribution on that day is managed by Day Area Committee (DAC) which corresponds to a day of the week. Users are grouped according to the day on which they are entitled to draw water. Farmer group elects a chairman to head the committee. The chairman chooses two more members from the group to help in water distribution management. They work out water scheduling and ensure that the farmers adhere to the same. Water schedules are not rigid and are flexible for adjustment. Allocation in the area commanded by *kundi* rests with the DAC. Farmers are expected to maintain field channels down below the *kundis*. Water efficiency naturally depends on availability of water from silt-removed cleaned field channels by the farmer community.

Scheduling of *kundi* operation and grouping of farmers rests with the Tubewells Area Management Committee (TAMC) which does the work with assistance of irrigation officials. Chairman of TAMC is elected by all the farmers in the command. A secretary and three members are picked up by the chairman with the consensus from the farmers. Junior engineer of irrigation is generally present at the time of formation of such committee. TAMC keeps liasion between farmers and the department. Its resolutions are expected to be acted upon by the government. The committee is also responsible for enforcing discipline in water sharing among the farmers. Norms for water allocation are drawn after thorough deliberations. Violation of the norms are recorded in the proceedings of the committee. Criminal offences are lodged in the police. Thus, DAC and TAMC take care of water distribution.

West Bengal

In West Bengal, many tubewells were turned over to panchayats. The panchayats, in turn, have turned them over to the user groups for actual management, though the accounting is under the supervision of the panchayats. This is said to be successful. The comprehensive Area Development Corporation helps identify the location for different kinds and sizes of tubewells and assists in supplying inputs. Each tubewell irrigates 80-100 acres. Groups of farmers instal pumpsets, and sell the water a little cheaper than the market rate. They are nominally supervised by panchayats but each group works independently.

North Gujarat

Entrepreneur farmers get together and invest in tubewells, each of which irrigates 100-150 acres. Surplus water not required by members is sold out at Rs.18 an hour. There is a water market and sometimes a farmer has a choice of getting water from several outlets near his land. Subsidy in electricity rates for tubewells helped farmers to sink tubewells which also reduced water-logging at some places but in other areas, it reduced the water levels very drastically.

Another alternative model in Gujarat is that of tubewell companies. From 5 to 120 members having landholding in the command form an informal organization which is not registered. All promoters of the company enter into an agreement and elect a manager, open a bank account; all resources are internally generated. There is complete autonomy and self-governance, They run tubewells on community basis.

Andhra Pradesh

Mulkanoor Multipurpose Cooperative Society has made successful ventures in 14 villages by digging open tubewells. Each irrigates 3-5 acres and has 4-5 members. Loans are given with joint liability.

Bihar

In Bihar, Vaishali Small Farmers' Association (VAFSA) organizes groups of small farmers to instal and manage tubewells. There are now about 35 tubewells, each irrigating about 40 acres. The farmers, selected with the help of block officials, are those generally having less than 5 acres and thus small farmers. Their lands should be contiguous and those who are willing to form a farmers' group. This group makes an agreement with the bank for finance for the tubewell. The bank has less risk because initially the fund came from Norway and another from CAPART. Farmers pay back the loan in 5 years. The members of a group share the cost of running the tubewell on a per acre basis. Water is provided in turns by land area, and surplus water is sold to non-members at prevailing market rates. A group-leader arranges rotation, looks after maintenance of equipment, keeps record, and collects the costs from the farmers. The farmers clean out their own field channels, sometimes collectively. This model was institutionalized in Bihar because of few dedicated leaders.

Rajasthan

Social assessment study in groundwater management has been started in pilot areas under Rajasthan Water Sector Restructuring Project (RWSRP) assisted by the World Bank. World Bank will advance loan to the tune of Rs. 23 crore for social assessment. It involves identification of social issues with approach to community based groundwater management. The results of social assessment will form the basis to develop a strategy to involve local communities in the overall planning, implementing (including of structures and systems development) and monitoring the groundwater object. Community will be directly associated to improve groundwater levels by formation of village level committees at panchayat level. These committees will consist of local residents who will make efforts for creating awareness among farmers regarding falling water levels and creating structures for maintaining and improving water level. State-level federation of such societies will also be constituted along with a technical assistance group which has already started working. NGOs are also being associated in the restructuring of groundwater project.

Field Observations

1. Groundwater projects have a distinct cost advantage over the large irrigation projects specially in areas where rivers flow in plains like that of Uttar Pradesh.
2. Marginal and small farmers are able to benefit by community tubewells since individually they could not afford its expenditure due to high initial capital investment.
3. State's role becomes inevitable in providing irrigation to poorer farmers.
4. Association of community at field level below distributory definitely increases water efficiency, crop intensity, productivity, use of improved seeds and fertilizers as well as improved agricultural practices.

Difficulties

1. Poor utilization of water due to non-availability of power since tubewells are run by electricity only.
2. Lack of cooperation between irrigation officials and water users and hence lapses in water distribution system.
3. Absence of associating farmers at layout stage.
4. Agricultural extension services hardly coordinate with irrigation department for deciding agricultural crops and intensity of cultivation or improved practices based on availability of water.
5. Wasteful use of water due to poor maintenance of field channels by water users. Maintenance being a collective responsibility of the irrigators reflects poor participation of the people.
6. Price fixation ignores the cost considerations.
7. Irrigation officers do not bother to attend meetings of farmers to chalk out a common programme of action.
8. Uncertainties in water supply jeopardize a good agriculture programme.

On the whole, PTWs project was a success in view of economy in initial capital investment and increased individual and group gains in productivity and income caused by community participation though to the desired extent. Mutually respectful and responsive relationship between the department and the farmers alone can lead to better functioning of the system. Irrigation department should change its mindset of using farmers' committees as an extended arm of their own.

References

Clarence, Maloney and Raju, K.V., *Managing Irrigation Together*, Sage Publications, New Delhi, 1994.

Hooja, Rakesh, Ganesh Pangare and Raju, K.V., *Users in Water Management*, Rawat Publications, Jaipur and New Delhi, 2002.

Satish, S. and Sundar, A., *People's Participation and Irrigation Management*, Commonwealth Publishers, New Delhi, 1990.

10

Community Management of Drinking Water

Drinking water is a strange boon of nature. But it is an irony that although three-fourth of the earth is water, only 1 per cent of the total water reserve is fresh water. Nevertheless, if properly harnessed, even this 1 per cent is sufficient to meet the drinking water and other needs of the global population. Once upon a time people drank water through natural fountains and rivers, which flow from mountains. With increase in population, when water resources became exhausted or became dry due to lesser rainfall, rulers excavated underground *baoris* and individual families constructed *tankas* for storage of rain water. *Baoris* were open for public from where women fetched water and used to bring to their homes. Individual families who had private *tankas*, collected rainwater from roof top or ground and stored it and even locked water tankas in desert areas. Such stored water was meant for use of individual families only. Surface water was also stored in dams and tanks and people also used tank water for drinking. But, such water was not potable and UNICEF surveys indicated that 80 per cent diseases spread due to unsafe drinking water. In desert areas, drinking water was supplied from far off dams through canals. Such water was made potable through the process of filtration. Wherever groundwater was available, tubewells were dug for supply of drinking water through overhead tanks and pipelines. In small villages, handpumps were dug for supply of water to hamlets and small villages. But all such arrangements for construction and maintenance of drinking water-works have so far been the sole responsibility of the state. Though people are happy to get piped water supply in their homes, but it is due to centralized management. Along with tubewell, high level tank is constructed, network of pipeline is spread over the whole area, every house is fitted with a metre and a valve. To control such systems, officers are appointed, staff and linemen are engaged, bills are issued and water charges are collected. The control of water is centralized in hands of a monopolist state agency. Inequalities creep in. People in big cities get 150 litres per capita per day whereas villagers do not get even 40 litres per capita per day which is considered as minimum requirement of a living being. The poor people in rural areas do not get water even for drinking, whereas richer section of society get water even for their lawns in big cities. Such inequalities must be removed in a democracy.

On the other side, water supply agency complains that the water rates were kept quite low, maintenance cost has increased due to high pay scales of public servants, cost of construction, pipes, motors and electricity is ever increasing and huge cash losses are incurred on account of water supply to people. Now, since the population has increased tremendously and it is spread over a number of cities, towns and more than 5 lakh villages, it has become a herculian task for the state to manage drinking water supply. Per capita supply of water has reduced. Even in cities and towns, due to ever decreasing groundwater levels, water is not supplied daily. There are towns which get water supply every second or even every fourth day. Huge funds are required to meet public demand for water, specially in rural areas. Resources of the state are dwindling, working staff is also not sincere enough to attend to public complaints promptly and expectations of the public are very high in a democratic system of governance.

Public water supply system is suffering from following problems:

- Charges for supply of water are too low. Hence, people use same water for cattle, for lawns, for flush latrines and miscellaneous washing purposes extravagantly.
- Government has no surplus funds for new investment in augmenting water supply sources as per increasing requirements of people. Whatever taxes are recovered, they are exhausted in salary bills of employees.
- Staff as well as public do not take any interest in preventing leakage of water from pipelines and taps.
- Government staff is not competent to manage the affairs efficiently.
- Rich people, influential elite and political bosses do not allow rates to increase to meet the deficit.
- Poor people do not get water because nobody cares for them. Leaders as well as bureaucrats are interested in huge commission from works rather than poor persons.

Problems have arisen because of low water rates and maladministration of officials.

The wave of privatization is spreading throughout the globe. International agencies like the World Bank are also pressing the states to privatize drinking water supply also. After privatization, water will also be sold like vegetables. Technical progress has changed the very nature of supply of drinking water. Nobody likes to fetch water from public taps or tubewells, but water reaches every house through pipeline. Women are also happy to get water through taps in their kitchen and bathroom itself. Moreover, 80 per cent diseases which used to infect children due to unsafe drinking water from open tanks and wells, have also reduced considerably.

But, after water supply from tubewells, traditional sources like *baoris, tankas*, wells have become out of use. Not more than 30 per cent rainwater is utilized for irrigation, whereas 70 per cent goes waste in nallahs and rivers which could be alternatively used for irrigation through 'contour bunding' of fields and construction of 'check dams' for storage of rainwater and raising groundwater levels in the area.

Is Privatization Advisable?

The World Bank feels that after transfer of water supply arrangement to private hands, it will run on commercial basis. Leakage and wastage of drinking water will be prevented. Water metres will be in working condition. Adjustment of reading by water metre reader will be no more. Theft of water will be prevented. Private supplier will take loan for augmenting sources of water, hence will like to recover the invested amount. But will poor people get relief?

The Way Out

Examples of privatization of water supply in Argentina and France are before us to take lesson. The supplier in Argentina increased water rates from 24 peso to 59 peso within a few years. Vivendi – the private company in France – invested funds borrowed from the French government only and did not invest even a single pie of its own. People were enraged and even resorted to strike. Vivendi flew away from the town.

To learn from these experiences, the following way out is suggested:

- Strict government control on pricing of water supply must be kept along with privatization.
- Water Tribunal must be created to settle disputes regarding fixing of water rates and hearing complaints of poor people regarding non-supply of water in their areas.
- Private person or company share of investment in augmentation must be specified in advance and strictly adhered to.

The interest of poor people regarding supply of optimum water in their areas and reasonable water rates can protect the interest of society in the above system.

National Drinking Water Mission

A national water supply and sanitation programme was introduced in the social welfare sector in the year 1954. The Government of India provided assistance to the states to establish special investigation divisions in the Fourth Five-Year Plan to carry out identification of the problem villages. Taking into account the magnitude of the problem and to accelerate the pace of coverage of problem villages, the central government introduced the Accelerated Rural Water Supply Programme (ARWSP) in 1972-73 to assist the states with 100 per cent grants-in-aid to implement the schemes in the villages. This programme continued till 1973-74. But, with the introduction of the Minimum Needs Programme (MNP) during the Fifth Five-Year Plan (1974-75) period, it was withdrawn. The programme was, however, reintroduced in 1977-78 when the progress of supply of safe drinking water to the identified problem villages under the MNP was not found to be satisfactory.

The entire programme was given a 'mission' approach when Technology Mission on Drinking Water Management, also called the National Drinking Water Mission (NDWM), was introduced as one of the five societal missions in 1986. It was renamed after the name of Rajiv Gandhi in 1991.

Following were the objectives of NDWM in 1986:

- cover 1,37,155 residual problem villages as on 1 April 1986 with safe drinking water;
- evolve appropriate technology mix;
- improve performance and cost effectiveness of the ongoing programmes;
- create awareness on the use of safe drinking water; and

- take conservation measures for the sustained supply of water.

ARWSP continued during the Eighth as well as the Ninth Five-Year Plan period. Due to lack of sufficient funds and re-emergence of 'not covered habitations' ARWSP continued.

Need for Change

The strategies of rural water supply programme hitherto adopted revolved round the basic premise that provision of safe drinking water is the responsibility of the government. A change in the technology focus to hand pumps fitted on tubewells and borewells had resulted in an impressive increase in total rural water supply coverage. However, the availability of potable drinking water in rural area, specially during the summer months, is still not satisfactory. Even though, about one lakh habitations are covered every year, the number of problem habitations has not declined proportionately. The reasons identified for uncovered villages were:

- Fast depletion of groundwater level, which also increases incidence of quality problems of arsenic and flouride, etc.
- Sources go dry and defunct due to deforestation with consequent reduced recharge and lack of protection.
- Heavy emphasis on new construction and poor attention to maintenance.
- Non-involvement of people in operations and maintenance.
- Neglect of traditional water management practices.

Revised guidelines in Ninth Plan stressed the control on over extraction of groundwater, more funds for repairs and rehabilitation, increasing people's participation, water to be treated as a socio-economic good and stronger links with watershed development programmes. Prime object was to cover all rural habitations and reach the unreached with access to safe drinking water. Norms for providing potable drinking water are 40 litres per capita per day (lpcd) for humans to meet the needs of drinking, cooking, bathing, washing and ablution, 30 lpcd for animals in hot and cold desert ecosystem. With normal output of 12 litres per minute, one handpump or stand post is estimated for every 250 persons. In case of independent habitation, an independent source is to be provided even for lesser population.

- A rural habitation not having any safe drinking water source, with a permanently settled population of 20 households or 100 persons, whichever is more, may be taken as a unit for coverage with funds under ARWSP.
- Desert areas and SC/ST habitations with less than 100 persons can, however, be covered under the ARWSP.
- The distance between two sources should not be more than 1.6 km in plains and 100 metre elevation in hills. Conference of state ministers in-charge of rural water supply, held on 19-20 October 2001, relaxed the norms of coverage to 55 lpcd in place of 40 lpcd, distance 0.5 km in place of 1.6 km and height 50 metre elevation in place of 100 metre but relaxed norms will be applicable after all rural habitations are covered as per old norms.
- Habitations, which have a water source but are affected with quality problem such as excess salinity, iron, fluoride, arsenic or other toxic elements or biologically contaminated, shall not be treated as covered.
- If quantity of water is not sufficient to meet drinking and cooking needs.
- Priority is given to SC/ST habitations or having larger SC/ST population.
- Coverage of schools and *anganwadis* where safe drinking water could not be provided.
- There should be women caretakers for handpumps in the habitations.
- Certificate about satisfactory completion of the schemes may be obtained from women groups in the habitations.

- Prominent women from the habitations should be represented on the village-level monitoring committees.

Experience has shown that wherever women are involved in such consultation and in maintenance of the sources, the performance of supply systems has been effective. Annual action plans are to be prepared six months in advance before the financial year starts.

Community Participation in Rural Drinking Water Supply

Janta Jal Yojna

Rajasthan government initiated 'Janta Jal Yojna' (People's Water Supply Scheme) in March 1994. It was experienced that governmentalization had been increasing day by day, whereas no effort was made for participation of consumers in drinking water schemes. If participation of people increases in schemes, then success would definitely be more. Janta Jal Yojna (JJY) could be sanctioned in villages where there is no source of drinking water or drinking water is insufficient as per norms of PHED.

- If any panchayat or village water committee proposes to make drinking water available to people from any well, PHED will reimburse electricity bill payable to the State Electricity Board in this behalf.
- Department can also deepen such wells as per requirement.
- Department will also give grant for repairs of motor used for drawal of drinking water. In seven desert districts where water is deeper, motor is installed by the department itself.
- Sanctioning power was also decentralized. Sanction is to be accorded by district-level committee, consisting of collector and superintending engineer of PHED.
- There is no government operator for such schemes. Part-time operator is engaged by community. It can also be run on contract basis.

- Committee can also give domestic connections and it is authorized to recover monthly water rates from such consumers. Total income from JJY belongs to village committee only.
- Such schemes can be sanctioned for villages having population of 500 and above.

As per progress report of PHED for the year 2002-03, following JJY schemes are under operation by community:

Piped Schemes	357
Pump and Tank Schemes	879
Regional Schemes	678
Total	1894

Aapni Yojna

Democracy	For the People By the People Of the People
Aapni Yojna	For the User By the User Of the User

It is a global rural water supply project of unusual size and complexity. The project area covers about 20,000 kms. It is implemented by the community with the help of NGO partners under the guidance of German consultants. Community Participation Unit (CPU) was established in 1994 by a consortium of five leading NGOs with the aim to carry out Aapni Yojna (Our Scheme), an integrated rural water supply, sanitation and health education programme covering 956 villages and 11 urban areas of three districts of Churu, Jhunjhunu and Hanumangarh of Rajasthan. It is funded by Government of India, Government of Germany and Government of Rajasthan. The present phase I covers a population of 9 lakhs in 370 villages and two towns of Taranagar and Sardar Shahr.

Sustainable supply of water is ensured from Indira Gandhi Canal as groundwater is insufficient and saline. The project includes raw water storage from feeder canal, treatment plant, pumping stations and 1,100 mm pipelines, clear water reservoir, booster pumping station, elevated reservoir and cluster network of pipelines for different villages. Public stand posts and cattle water troughs are constructed in villages as part of the project.

Framework of participation is at various levels. First participation bond was between governments of Germany and Government of Rajasthan. The Government of Rajasthan created special cell called Project Management Cell (PMC) from Public Health Engineering Department. A separate post of Chief Engineer was created for smooth execution and fast decision-making. Second participation bond was among leading five NGOs of Rajasthan for implementing community participation, sanitation, health education and women participation components of the project. Third participation bond is between the government and the NGO functionaries working closely with each other from down to top level, sharing each other's information and removing difficulties and working in a conducive environment. The role of German and Indian consultants is positive in supporting the work and creating the information channel between technical and social wings of this project. Fourth and important participation bond is between the project staff and the community. The regular interaction of CPU field staff with community has developed trust among the community for this project. The field intervention has empowered the village level community for managing their internal system independently. The communities are enthusiastically participating in all activities of the project.

Main Objectives

The main objectives of community development through community participation and the implementation of activities are as under:

- Reduction of wastage of water.
- Contribution by the community towards cost recovery.
- To create awareness and responsibility for the consumption of water.
- To implement the construction of low cost sanitation facilities.
- To launch women development activities and to promote family welfare measures.
- To implement ad-hoc measures according to a particular situation in the villages.

Limitations of Earlier Water Supply Projects

- Inadequate time for overall planning.
- Political interference in technical planning.
- Lack of exposure to the engineers in the use of quality techniques in project design and execution.
- Lack of supervision.
- Absence of cost recovery concept.
- Communities not involved in design and execution.
- Absence of community participation.
- Beneficiary women who suffer most in fetching water from far off locations, are not encouraged to participate in planning at the village level.
- Grossly inadequate logistics support to executing agencies.

Key Features of Aapni Yojna

Technical Features

- Four water treatment plants with total capacity of 8,550 m/hr capacity.
- Two raw water reservoirs with total capacity of 2.4 MCM.
- 1,100 mm PSCC and 900 mm PSCC pipeline covering a distance of 93.5 km and 36.5 km respectively.
- Eight pumping stations.

- Dedicated 33 KV electrical grid and sub-stations for the project.
- Voice communication system.
- Project area has been divided into several clusters depending on the topography and water demand of the villages.
- 24-hour supply is ensured from a strategically located service reservoir in a given cluster.
- One PSP is given for 150 human population of census 1991.
- Water supply norms: human – 40 lpcd, cattle – 30 lpcd (rural), 90 lpcd (urban).

Community Participation: Features

- Village-level Water and Health Committees (WHCs) have been formed and a contract signed between PMC, PHED and WHC.
- WHCs are involved in site selection of PSPs and CWTs.
- WHC arranges voluntary labour for trench excavation inside the village to build ownership of the scheme.
- Village level installations are taken care of by the WHC.
- Project Management Cell (PMC) attends to technical problems in each village.
- Water metre has been provided to each village and the water consumed in a month is billed to village WHC.
- WHC collects money from the village and deposits it with PMC.
- The Government of Rajasthan has sanctioned a special tariff structure for Aapni Yojna.

Water Distribution Management Activities in a Village

Step-wise activities are as under:

- Environment building for project acceptance. Group meetings with males and females in every locality where role and responsibility of people is clarified.

- Village general meeting and WHC formation having proper representation of women and weaker sections. WHC consists of communicator, sanitation representative, payment collector, caretaker and woman representative.
- WHC orientation and job distribution, clarifying their roles and responsibilities, maintaining records, etc.
- Social mapping for selecting sites for PSPs and CWTs.

Implementation Phase

- WHC conducts a census of the village, total family members and cattle for devising payment model. Census is updated every six months.
- Payment model for water charges according to which every household pays water charges as per the number of family members and cattle.
- Security money collection for one month advance is deposited with PMC.
- Site selection for PSP and CWT is done by WHC with the help of villagers. First, women group selects the sites, then WHC discusses and approves. PMC engineers check the technical feasibility and prepare layout for pipe laying and construction.
- Community arrange voluntary labour for trench digging. Project pays the money but it remains in corpus fund to be used for future maintenance.
- Construction work is done by PMC. Testing is done and after installation of village meter, the system is handed over to WHC.
- Community level training of WHC members is conducted regarding stand post attendants, water distribution management issues like record keeping, fault reporting, water charge collection and operation and maintenance of internal water supply system. A caretaker is trained for

internal maintenance of the system and given one tool-box from the project.

- In the follow-up phase, CPU monitors the proper use and maintenance of water supply installations.
- CPU monitors depositing of monthly bills regularly. Incase any village fails to deposit, CPU analyzes the problem and supports the villagers in solving the problem.

Project Benefits

- Availability of safe and potable water.
- Availability for 24 hours.
- Supply with adequate pressure.
- Collection of water charges by 'Pani Panchayat'.
- O&M with 'Pani Panchayat'.
- No wastage of water.
- 100 per cent recovery of water charges.
- Women's empowerment.
- Community participation.

Aapni Yojna, the first of its kind in the desert area, employs an innovative approach to integrate communities in all phases of the project from planning, decision-making, construction, O&M phase to organization and maintenance of the whole scheme. Assurance of regular availability of water at the nearest point all the 24 hours, reduction in irresponsible use and wastage of water, the good image of CPU and active role of village committees and a well defined payment model are substantially contributing to the success of the project. It is recognized by the householders themselves who are prepared to invest large sums of money on maintaining 'their own' facilities and regularly pay their water tariff. Even under severe drought, people's motivation to pay for water is not weakening at all. However, their ample understanding of the benefits makes all the difference. Beneficiaries are convinced of the necessity and advantages of safe drinking water and sanitation and its direct link to the reduction of water-borne diseases.

CPU's dedicated efforts are manifested in 168 villages connected with water supply, where villages through their water and health committees, women groups and user groups are involved in management, collection of water charges from households, village internal maintenance, fault reporting, record keeping, construction of sanitary package with active involvement of women and taking care of water supply facilities. These villages, which were worst affected with the scarcity of water, are now getting safe drinking water supply round the clock.

Renovation of Traditional Sources of Drinking Water

Programme of renovation of traditional water sources like wells and *baoris* was started from the year 2000. Such sources had become outdated because they had remained out of use since long. They could serve as useful source during drought periods. Panchayati Raj Institutions (PRIs) execute this programme. Works are selected at Zila Parishad level by district level committee. During two years (between 2000 and 2002), 32,303 such works were sanctioned out of which 18,532 were completed. Around 75 per cent funds are received from the central government and balance is supplemented by the state or community.

Sector Reform Pilot Projects

The Sector Reform Project was introduced on pilot basis with effect from April 1999 in rural water supply sector for institutionalizing community participation and to ensure sustainability of systems and sources. It was mainly because water is today perceived by the rural public as a social right, to be provided free by the government, rather than as a scarce resource which must be managed locally as a socio-economic good in order to ensure its effective use. This perception has grown out of the fact that the present rural water supply systems are designed and executed by the government departments/boards and imposed on end-users. Demand preferences of the people are not taken into account while executing the schemes. Experience has shown that supply driven approach has led to failure of a large number of water supply systems/ schemes.

There is a general recognition that that a transformation from a target-based, supply-driven approach which pays little attention to preferences of end-users, to a demand-based approach where users get the service they want and are willing to pay for is urgently required. Implementation of a participatory demand-driven approach will ensure that the public obtain the level of service they desire and can afford to pay. Further, full cost recovery of operations and maintenance and replacement costs will ensure the financial viability and sustainability of the schemes.

Conditions under which the people would be willing to maintain and operate water supply schemes

- Provided they own the scheme.
- If they have themselves installed the hand pump, or being actively involved throughout.
- If they have been trained to do simple repairs.
- If they and not the government maintain the asset.
- If they have sufficient funds for maintenance.
- If they have to pay for O&M.

Main Features

- Adoption of a demand-driven approach based on empowerment of villagers to ensure their full participation in the project through a decision-making role in the choice of scheme design and management arrangement.
- Focus on village level capacity building.
- Ensure an integrated approach to water supply, sanitation and hygiene promotion.

- At least 10 per cent capital cost sharing and 100 per cent sharing of O&M cost by users. Proportion of capital cost would be 15 per cent if villagers with population below 1,500 adopt pipe and tank (P&T) in place of hand pump or piped water supply instead of P&T if population is less than 4,000. Participatory contribution would be 20 per cent if instead of 40 lpcd they want 70 lpcd in their village. Contribution could be in the form of cash, or in kind of labour, land or material.
- Using NGOs and alternative service providers.
- Building and implementing consensus on key policy and institutional reforms.
- Targeting the poorest and most vulnerable groups.
- Considerable degree of flexibility in choosing the appropriate institutional model for service delivery suited to their own local context.
- Taking up of conservation measures for sustained supply of water through rainwater harvesting and groundwater recharge structures.

Sector Reform as a Process Different from "Business as Usual"

- Decentralized institutional framework
- Demand responsive approach
- Need to understand community perspective
- Need to reform delivery mechanisms to become facilitators and not providers
- Need for capacity development at all levels

Capacity-building much more than training alone covers:

- Technology
- Society
- Organizations
- Institutions

Elements of capacity Development

1. Skills and knowledge – We are able to do
2. Attitudes and motivation – We are willing to do
3. Enabling environment – We can do

Objectives

- To reach a common understanding of principles and processes among key stakeholders
- To identify main bottlenecks in implementation at different levels
- To provide an organized and structured vision for capacity development
- To foment feeling of ownership

Is a participatory learning and planning process allowing us to:

- Think together
- Plan together
- Act together

Methodology

- Review sector reform and total sanitation principles and procedures
- Stakeholders analysis – present and future roles
- Preliminary identification of community development needs by stakeholders
- Field visits for validation and identification of obstacles
- Identification of main obstacles in reaching reform's main expected result
- Linking stakeholders community development needs to main expected results
- Development of a CD plan specific to the district
- Development of an action plan with advice of technical member in view of community needs

- Getting consent of the community for collection of water rates as per family members and cattle and in view of estimated expenditure on running and maintenance of the scheme
- Presentation of plans to village WSC and then to DWSC for sanction

Sanction of the Project

- Deposit community contribution in project account in the bank
- Receipt of first instalment from DRDA
- Issue of tenders as per technical specifications
- Consideration by the committee
- Accept tenders of approved contractor

Execution and Account Keeping

- Fixing responsibility of members of committee for inspecting quality of work and equipment
- Secretary to maintain accounts as per receipt and expenditure
- Review meetings of committee every week
- Submit utilization certificate of first instalment and second instalment for receipt of remaining amount
- Arrange for training of caretaker, mechanic for timely running of the scheme

Operation and Maintenance

- Appoint part-time operator/mechanic for running the scheme
- Collection of water rates per month in advance to pay electricity bill, minor repairs, wages and contingent expenditure
- Day-to-day monitoring to prevent misuse of water and optimum utilization of water resources

Sector reform scheme of community participation was adopted in 67 selected districts in 26 states of the country. Position was reviewed on 19 October 2001 in the State Ministers' Conference and it was found as under:

(Rs. in crores)

Year	*Projects Approved*	*Project Outlay*	*Community Contribution*	*Utilization*
1999-2000	42	1103.24	20.65	129.68
2000-01	15	587.46	12.82	66.66
2001-02	6	209.75	0.51	4.78
2002-03	4	160.00	1.28	0.16
Total	67	2060.45	35.26	201.72

Physical performance in these project districts was found as follows:

Number of VWSC constituted	22,203
VWSC Account opened	14,517
Habitations covered with IEC	38,095
Number of training conducted	4,995
Number of persons trained	2,23,388
Number of schemes taken up	22,108
Number of schemes in schools	5,983
Total number of schemes	28,091
Number of schemes completed	8,261
Number of schemes taken over by communities for O&M	6,782
Number of contributors	17,87,891

The experience of community participation was not very much encouraging as only 29 per cent schemes could be completed and 24 per cent were handed over to community for running and maintenance in following areas:

State	*District*	*Schemes completed*	*Schemes taken over*	*Remarks*
Andhra Pradesh	Khammamm	330	57	Satisfactory
	Chittoor	0	0	
	Nalgonda	0	0	
	Nellore	0	0	
	Prakasam	0	0	
	Guntur	0	0	
	East godavari	0	0	
Assam	Kamrup	38	38	Satisfactory
	Jorhat	0	0	
	Sonitpur	0	0	
Jammu & Kashmir	Srinagar	14	14	Satisfactory
	Udhampur	59	0	
Madhya Pradesh	Gwalior	121	91	Good
	Sehore	0	0	
	Hoshangabad	108	108	Very Good
	Narsinghpur	109	109	
	Raisen	32	32	
Orissa	Sunder Garh	226	219	Good
	Balasore	185	0	
	Ganjam	1	1	
	Ganjam	1	1	
Tamil Nadu	Coimbatore	1017	1017	Very Good
	Cuddalore	397	397	
	Perambalur	406	282	
	Vellore	1998	1998	
	Kancheepuram	0	0	
	Virudhunagar	0	0	
Tripura	West Tripura	2301	2301	Very Good
West Bengal	Midnapur	110	110	Very Good
	N.24.Parganas	0	0	Very Good
Arunachal Pradesh	West Siang	6	0	Poor
Haryana	Karnal	452	6	Poor
	Yamuna Nagar	230	0	

Contd...

Contd...

State	*District*	*Schemes completed*	*Schemes taken over*	*Remarks*
Himachal Pradesh	Sirmour	26	0	Poor
Karnataka	Bellary	4	1	Poor
	Magalore	42	0	
	Mysore	0	0	
Kerala	Kasaragod	0	0	Poor
	Kollam			
Maharashtra	Amravati	1	0	Poor
	Raigad	42	0	
	Dhule	0	0	
	Nanded	0	0	
Mizoram	Serchhip	1	0	Poor
Punjab	Bhatinda	0	0	Poor
	Moga	0	0	
	Muktsar	0	0	
Rajasthan	Alwar	1	1	Poor
	Rajsamand	0	0	
	Jaipur	0	0	
	Sikar	0	0	
Sikkim	Sikkim South	0	0	Poor
	Sikkim West	0	0	
Uttar Pradesh	Agra	0	0	Poor
	Chandauli	0	0	
	Lucknow	0	0	
	Mirzapur	0	0	
	Sonebhadra	0	0	
Uttranchal	Haridwar	0	0	Poor
Jharkhand	Dhanbad	0	0	
Meghalaya	Ri-Bhoi	0	0	
Nagaland	Dimapur	0	0	
Total		8261	6782	
Total		28091		
Schemes		28091		
Sanctioned		29.41 per cent	24.14 per cent	

As evident from the above performance, Madhya Pradesh, Tamil Nadu, Tripura and West Bengal were four out of 26 states which showed good success of the pilot project.

Swajaldhara Projects

After successful experiment of sector reform participatory rural water supply project in 67 pilot districts, participatory and community-led 'Swajaldhara' was launched as a reform initiative throughout the country from 25 December 2002. United Nations General Assembly has also declared year 2003 the 'International Year of Fresh Water'. The role of governments has to shift from service provider to that of facilitator for providing financial and policy support to the communities and their institutions for fulfilling the desired levels of services on a sustainable and equitable basis. The emphasis is to be shifted to conducting mass media campaign to create awareness about the need and benefit of reforms amongst the opinion makers and development practitioners. There is increasing awareness of the need to strengthen technical and managerial capacity of different tiers of local governments and the communities for implementing different and diverse models of service delivery.

There is global consensus that "management at the lowest appropriate level" is an important prerequisite for sustainability. The strategy has changed from the top-down, fully government implemented approach in Maharashtra to a community participation approach to Karnataka through a "demand responsive approach in partnership with NGOs and user groups" in Uttar Pradesh, and finally to "community-driven development" in Kerala and Karnataka. The successive projects show the evolution of key strategies needed to improve sustainability. The World Bank-assisted Rural Water Supply and Sanitation Project (popularly known as *swajal* (pure water) in Uttar Pradesh has been acknowledged nationally and internationally as the best practice example in implementing a demand responsive approach.

Key Elements of Swajaldhara

1. Demand-driven and community participation approach.
2. Panchayats/communities to plan, implement, operate, maintain and manage all drinking water schemes.
3. Partial capital cost sharing by the communities upfront in cash and to be deposited with DIA before issue of 50 per cent as first instalment.
4. Full ownership of drinking water assets with Gram Panchayats.
5. Full operation and maintenance (O&M) by the users/ panchayats. Gram Panchayats and blocks adopting the reforms principles will be eligible for Swajaldhara projects.
6. Beneficiary group should be a registered society and would submit proposal through Gram Panchayat or Block Panchayat as the case may be.
7. Ten per cent of the estimated capital cost of the schemes (5% in case of villages having 50% population of SC/ST as per 2001 census).
8. Contribution in cash is paid to the implementing agency (Zila Parishad).
9. State Water and Sanitation Mission (SWSM) will engage the existing agency undertaking rural drinking water supply programmes and will be termed as District Implementing Agencies (DIA).
10. DIA would be responsible for the formulation, implementation and management of the project.
11. DIA will select agencies and release the funds to Block Panchayat/Gram Panchayat/village water and sanitation committee and be responsible for proper management of funds.
12. DIA will sanction the scheme and enter into bipartite/tripartite agreements with executing agency.
13. Providing water supply facilities in schools and habitations with water scarcity and revival of traditional water sources to ensure drinking water sustainability can also be

implemented under Swajaldhra. Application will however have to be made and DIA will send its views.

14. One-time O&M grant will be given as revolving fund after running the scheme within six months. It will be on case to case basis.

Block Panchayat/Gram Panchayat/VWSC/BG will be responsible for:

- Execution of sanctioned schemes;
- Place the progress of scheme implementation in each Gram Sabha meeting;
- Ensure community participation in scheme activities;
- Arrange community contribution towards capital cost in cash;
- Open and manage bank accounts for management of project funds;
- Procure construction material/goods and select contractors for construction activities;
- Supervise construction activities;
- After release of 50 per cent as first installment, next instalment will be payable after 60 per cent fund of previous instalment has been utilized as per audited report;
- Commission and take over completed water supply works;
- Collect funds and manage O&M of water supply works; and
- Submit progress report to DIA within 10 days of the succeeding month.

Ground Reality

Due to age long practice of spoon feeding the villagers since independence, it will take a very long time to bring attitudinal change in mindset of people living in rural areas. Departmental hold on contractors and traders will hardly allow village level committees to implement schemes independently. Moreover, technical dependence on PHED engineers for preparing project and ensuring quality material as well as proper maintenance will still continue, in view of limited capacity building of village level committees. Voluntary work of collection of water charges and account keeping by villagers independently may result in more failures than success. Panchayats are also not equipped with competent staff to take over O&M responsibilities. Success story of 'Aapni yojna' of Churu district is also due to strong participation bonds between PHED Chief Engineer in project area, five leading NGOs, World Bank experts on site, facilitators for assistance of villagers in case problems arise. All over the country, such ideal conditions do not prevail nor any budget provision exists in Swajaldhara for capacity-building and human resource development.

Kothun (Chaksu Block, Jaipur District, Rajasthan)

Population	2,962 (expected 3,250)
Gram Sabha	20.5.2001
Committee Formation	20.5.2001
Registration of Committee	8.6.2001

Steps Taken

- Village contact campaign
- Survey of village
- User Group formation
- Formation of WATSAN committee and its registration
- Plan formulation for water sources
- Estimation of cost involved in works
- 10 per cent people's participation
- Opening bank account
- Receipt of first instalment from DRDA
- Construction of water source and pipelines
- Provide water to villagers
- Management and maintenance by community

Construction Works Undertaken

1. Open well (3 metre wide, 21.5 metre deep)
2. Pipeline 100 mm – 4,000 metres
   80 mm – 3,000 metres
3. High water tank capacity 1.25 lakh litres
4. Sanctioned amount – 19.57 lakh
5. Public contribution – 2.94 lakh
6. Executing Agency – Kothun village committee
7. Water connections – 80
8. Water charges per family – Rs.50 per month
   Scheme is being run by community successfully for the last two years without any difficulty.

Ojharia Village (District Churu, Rajasthan)

Village Ojharia is covered by water supply in 'Aapni Yojna'. It is a small Jat dominated village having 110 households. Village Health Committee of this village has been playing an active role in implementation of the project. One day something happened that tested the committee's strength and managing capability. A shepherd from a neighbouring non-project village came with 300 sheep at the cattle water trough of this village. Villagers informed him to pay charges to which shepherd agreed. However, a relative of the shepherd living in Ojharia asked him not to pay. He also refused to pay to committee members and even abused the committee members. He challenged the committee to extract payment from him.

The committee reported to police who asked them to bring the shepherd. It made him angry and that night he opened the tap deliberately and wasted water which flooded the streets. When a woman closed the tap, he abused the woman and again opened the tap. WHC noted the metre reading early morning and calculated the water wasted by him.

The committee reported the incident to Taranagar police station. The culprit was taken into custody. His relatives came to police station and reached an understanding with WHC.

They made the payment for water consumed and wasted, conveyance charges of the committee and the fine levied by WHC.

After this incident the water management system of the village is going on smoothly, the people come and make their monthly payments to the committee and take care that water is not wasted in their village. Because of the prompt and strong decision taken by the committee, this group has become an example of effective water management for other villages also.

Village Birmi Patta, Birmi Khalsa and Dantli (District Churu, Rajasthan)

These are tail-end villages of their cluster. One day a neighbouring village (of Bhadra tehsil not covered by the project) tapped the main line supplying water to these villages and attached a pipeline to their own village. As a result, water pressure decreased drastically in these villages. The people complained to the project monitoring committee about the drop in pressure. Even after many days no action was taken on their complaint.

The people of all these villages met and decided to tackle the problem themselves. They formed a surveillance team that patrolled the course of the main line from their village to the ESR. They located the point of tapping and cut off this illegal pipeline. In this way they restored the water supply to their villages by their own collective action.

Rajpuria Village (District Churu, Rajasthan)

Village Rajpuria has a mixed community of Jat, Brahmin, Nai, Nayak, Meghwal and Babaria castes. When the Community project unit started working in this village, the people were excluding one group, i.e., Babariyas from the project work. The reason for this was that Babariyas are nomadic, robbers and generally quarrelsome. It was felt that these people cannot participate in development work, and they would impede the work of the project.

On the basis of such convictions, the WHC was formed without representation from the Babariya caste. As project work progressed, the Babariyas remained indifferent. When security money was being collected, the villagers said that the Babariyas could not deposit security because they did not belong to the village. They were nomads. Nevertheless, the project staff kept up their efforts to convince the community to participate.

When the project work reached the last stage of voluntary labour when pipelines were laid for the water supply, it was the last opportunity for the Babariyas to join the project, but they were still not showing any interest. Fortunately, a boy of Babariya caste was contacted who was a matriculate, one Jat pipe-fitter and a Jat ex-Sarpanch made the last effort.

Another village meeting was organized and this time Babariyas also attended. This community was told that it was the last chance to get integrated with both the development work and rest of the village community. Unless they participated now, they would miss the chance to progress – other communities would develop and they would always remain isolated and backward.

They were stunned by this revelation. They finally agreed to accept the project. They paid the security money. Another PSP was constructed in their area and the community proceeded to dig for the pipeline extension to their *mohalla*. Today water management is still going on in the village with the participation of the whole community.

In recent past, governments have also started the practice of privatization of drinking water in favour of multinational companies after pressure from the World Bank. It has given rise to people's movement because monopoly of private companies is likely to exploit the water users by charging higher rates for water supply. Case of Vivendi Company of France is very recent. This company raised the water charges from 24 peso to 59 peso in few years and invested funds out of government loans. It had to run away due to hue and cry from the community.

Rajendra Singh, Magsaysay award winner, under the banner of 'National Water Brotherhood', organized wide rallies from 30 January 2003 to create awareness in the community against privatization of water and propagate for change in water policy so that water is treated as joint property of the government and the community.

A National Water Conference was also organized at Sewa Gram opposing the National Water Policy formulated by the Government of India regarding commercialization of water resource which was given by nature. The government was warned not to play with fundamental and birth right of people over water.

Panchayats of Kerala have even gone to the extent of organizing World Water Conference from 21 January 2004 and 'battle for water' is being fought between people and Coco-Cola company against overexploitation of groundwater. It was a historic victory for Perumatti Gram Panchayat (Kerala) when the Kerala High Court, on 16, December 2003, directed the Coco-Cola company to find out alternative sources of water for its bottling plant within a month. Gram Panchayat had cancelled its license in view of excess drawal of groundwater. Pepsi-cola is another target. Villagers, mostly Dalits and tribal people, are struggling for right to water. The struggle at Gram Panchayat, Plachimada (Kerala) is part of the worldwide struggle against transnational companies that exploit natural resources like water. Water belongs to the people. The new water policy of the government is geared towards privatization. Resistance against stealing of water from the common man is being globalized. The 'Plachimada Declaration', adopted at the end of the conference, emphasized that water is not a private property, not a commodity, but a common resource, a fundamental right of man. The right to conserve, use and manage water is fully vested with local community. This is the very basis of water democracy. Any attempt to reduce or deny this right is a crime. It is in such a background that the whole issue on community management of water has to be viewed now.

References

Achievements 2002, Community Participation Unit, Aapni Yojana, Integrated Water Supply, Sanitation and Health Education Programme in Churu, Jhunjhunu and Hanumangarh districts of Rajasthan (jointly funded project by the Government of Rajasthan and Government of Germany through KFW).

Conference of State Ministers of Rural Development on Rural Drinking Water, New Delhi, 5 December 2002.

George, Mathew, *Panchayati Raj Update*, Institute of Social Sciences, New Delhi, December 2003 and January 2004.

Indian Reform Initiatives in Water Sector, Key Note Address by M.Venkaiah Naidu at Water Forum 2002, World Bank, Washington, 6 May 2002.

Progress Report 2002-03, Public Health Engineering Department, Rajasthan.

Rajiv Gandhi National Drinking Water Mission, Ministry of Rural Development, Guidelines for Implementation of Rural Water Supply Programme.

Sector Reform Project Rajasthan – August 2002, Public Health Engineering Department.

11

Future Prospects and Policy

India has been a welfare state committed to democracy, development and decentralization of powers. People's participation has emerged as a key developmental strategy and it has been given a concrete shape in the form of Panchayati Raj Institutions (PRIs) in India. People's participation in formulation and implementation of rural development programmes has unfortunately not received the proper attention and importance it deserved.

Various programmes for development of rural areas as well as welfare measures for poor people have been implemented for more than 50 years but even then the improvement in their economic and social conditions is much below the accepted level. They must be motivated to play more active participatory role in the entire process and develop a greater degree of self-reliance and initiative. This raises following pertinent questions:

1. What are the reasons for lack of involvement of people in rural development programmes?
2. How can the participation of the people be obtained for their own welfare?

3. What are the loopholes and deficiencies in such programmes?
4. How can these be overcome?

The central government started community development programme in 1952 with the object of "development of the people, by the people, for the people". Infrastructure development in the form of rural roads, school buildings, community drinking water wells, small irrigation tanks, etc., was undertaken with the help of community. Large funds were invested but looking to the vast areas and multiple needs, it could satisfy only part of the requirements of rural areas. To some extent, physical development for the people was done through community development programme.

Regarding development of the people, schools were opened in rural areas in large numbers for making rural people literate. In spite of total literacy campaigns in the country, literacy levels are much lower than expected. In health sector also, primary health centres have been opened for average population of 30,000 and health sub-centre for average population of 5,000, but due to non-availability of doctors and paramedical staff in rural areas, health services are not reaching the poor and needy people. Quality of services are below satisfaction.

Though there was a provision for *shramdaan* or 'community share' in local development programme, but direct involvement of people in planning as per field requirements was absent. It was in 1959 when the era of 'Panchayati Raj' ushered in the process of direct people's participation was possible at village, block and district levels where institutions of Gram Panchayat, Panchayat Samiti and Zila Parishad respectively were constituted. Villagers had an opportunity to participate in the planning process through Gram Sabha at village level and execute works of rural development through Gram Panchayats and Panchayat Samitis. There was great enthusiasm among non-officials as well as officers regarding fulfilling people's needs through speedy implementation of local development programmes.

Economic development has not reached one-third population as yet. To the extent that 36 per cent rural families are still below poverty line and do not earn Rs. 20,000 per annum for an average family of 5-6 members as per Tenth Plan document. The Government of India started District Rural Development Agencies (DRDAs) in every district in 1978 to implement poverty alleviation and rural employment programmes as part of national policy. However, we have not been able to ensure fair wage or living wage as per Article 43 of Directive Principles of State Policy enunciated in Constitution of India.

Panchayati Raj provided good training ground for political leaders. Sarpanchas became Pradhans, Pradhans became Ministers, Pramukhs became Chief Ministers and members of Parliament and so on and so forth. Interest of elected representatives was more towards their personal benefit and political advancement rather than participation in 'planning from below' and real economic development of masses in general and poorer sections of the community in particular.

Government Programme: Not People's Programme

PRIs were constituted primarily with the purpose of associating people's representatives in planning at the base level as well as ensuring community participation in execution of rural development works and their maintenance in subsequent period. But people generally treated development works as government works. Village works were never owned by them. Community development programme could become development programme 'for the people' but it could never become development programme 'of the people'. It has been realized that people's participation has been lacking to the desired extent while implementing rural development programmes. Efforts were made, to involve people by way of 'public contribution' in 1952 and by way of Panchayati Raj in 1959 but active involvement of the community could not be achieved. The real poor is still cornered and helpless.

Village Level Committees

Latest efforts in the arena of people's participation have been made by forming village level committees for development and management of social forestry, water conservation, agricultural development, animal husbandry development, training of self-help groups of poorer sections and women. Management committees are also executing and maintaining community lift irrigation schemes. In such development programmes, people at grassroots level are being involved but they look more for personal benefits rather than for the general good. All are concerned as how to ensure active people's participation in rural development works at village level.

Demands of ever increasing population has raised demand for fuel, fodder and food grains. There is a big question mark regarding government management of lands, forests and water resources. Hence, serious effort is essential so that management of natural resources meets the basic requirements of people on an equitable basis without causing environmental damage.

Both the Forest Conservation Act, 1980 and Indian Forest Act, 1927 provided for management of common property resources. Article 39 (B) of the Constitution of India provides that the control of material resources of the community are so distributed so as to best subserve the common good. Likewise, the National Forest Policy, 1988 and the National Water Policy, 1987 have also acknowledged the importance of common property resources and common lands.

The National Water Policy, 1987 mentions that "economic development and activities including agriculture, industrial and urban development should be planned with due regard to constraints imposed by configuration of water availability. There should be a water zoning of the country and economic activities should be guided and regulated in accordance with such zoning".

The National Forest Policy, 1988 also stressed that "village and community lands including those on foreshores and environs of tanks not required for other productive uses should be taken up for development of tree crops and fodder resources..."

Technical Community on Drought Prone Area Programme and Desert Development Programme (1994), while recommending development on watershed basis also opined that "since the objective of watershed development is ecological improvement and conservation of natural resources as well as socio-economic development of local population, watershed management efforts must incorporate soil and water conservation and land use planning into a broader framework that takes into consideration not only physical interrelationship but economic, social and institutional factors as well.... Appropriate arrangements should be made for distribution of benefits to watershed community from the government lands and watershed development."

Equal Rights to all Sections of the Community

Common property resources like village pastures, community forests, village tanks, waste lands, waste dumping places, watershed drainage, rivers and rivulets, river beds and even groundwater are resources accessible to the whole community. Every individual has equal right to share its benefits and there are even legal provisions to such effect. But it is observed in practice that some influential persons monopolize the benefits and the interest of the poor is sacrificed. The voice of the poor remains unheard or it is a voice in wilderness. Hence, efficient land and water management is of crucial importance in the face of land and water being limited in supply and claimants of land and water being numerous. With liberalized economic policy and competitive economic development, the management of natural resources is at stake.

Participative Management by the Community

Hence, the Government of India in the Ninth Plan (1992-97) document acknowledged that "developmental activities undertaken with people's active participation have greater chances of success.... The role of the government should be to facilitate the process of people's involvement in developmental activities by creating the right type of institutional infrastructure, primarily in rural areas".

We cannot live without nature but its resources are not unlimited. Hence, we cannot extract them beyond certain limits. A constant extracting process of natural resources has caused their depletion which has polluted not only the environment but has also upset the ecological balance in the biosphere. The environment and ecological problems arising out of depletion of natural resources are not specific only to a country or nation but to the whole globe. Hence, immediate measures are needed for preservation, management and development of natural resources.

Natural resources cannot be managed and preserved properly without involving rural communities which derive their sustenance from natural resources. Role of communities is to manage natural resources in an optimum manner. Participation of people in shaping their destiny is the essence of democratic governance. People can understand their best interest and specially guard against interest of the poor provided they keep the community really in the forefront. People-centred and people-managed paradigm of development has been gaining popularity in recent years. In view of the changing scenario at global, national and regional levels, development must now be radically reviewed. It must be 'development around people' and not 'people around development'. It should empower people in view of democracy as prevailing system of governance.

These are really the basic principles to seek people's willing cooperation and real participation in all programmes relating to conservation, management and development of natural resources. People's potential, of course, has to be developed by increasing their capacity and capabilities through education, training and continuous participation at all stages of planning and execution. Natural resources are best conserved when people dependent on them for their survival are keenly involved in their management and conservation. Recent years have therefore witnessed an increasing accent on community based natural resource management at national as well as international levels. Community-based natural resource management is characterized by increased partnership with the community through community based organizations.

In the above context, people-centred and people-controlled paradigm of development has acquired new urgency in present times. In view of changing scenario at global, national and regional level, development must now be radically reviewed and revised. It must be woven around people who should be empowered. The World Development Report (1992) opined that projects are more successful if they are participatory in design and implementation. Involvement of people in a project at all levels gives them a sense of ownership which in turn makes them accountable.

People's participation presumes following features:

- Centrality of people is the essence of participation. Any programme should be based on felt-needs of people.
- People themselves should analyze their condition and propose the project.
- Capacity-building should be done to develop local capacity and mobilize local resources. People's potential can be increased by improving their capabilities through education, training and participation in developmental activities.
- Indigenous technical knowledge, technique and local methods should be valued.

- Marginalized classes must be associated and encouraged to participate actively.
- Women should also be included as equal partners.
- People should be taken into confidence that they are real planners, and benefits will also accrue to them in the short run and long run.
- People must be associated in execution and monitoring also.

The natural resources which are a boon of nature to mankind but they had been controlled by the state government departments of revenue, forest, irrigation, fisheries, public health engineering, etc., for earning revenues for the state, were badly managed in the past. Poor people were denied its benefits which were monopolized by few landlords, big farmers, contractors, industrialists and influential sections of society. Hence, now it is high time to vest back these natural resources to the people themselves through Gram Sabha or user committees for proper management, preservation and development to the optimum possible extent and to the best interest of the community as a whole including poor and marginalized classes.

Moreover, the resources on which people subsist for their living cannot be treated as property, that the people have an inherent natural right over the same as a means of livelihood which is superior to state's claim. The idea of inalienable right of the people to use resources for their livelihood, the questioning of displacement for development which essentially means alternative use of resources, the right of self-governance lose much of their significance without command over the habitat. Concentration of wealth and economic power goes against the constitutional provision of Article 39 which enjoins the state the responsibility to ensure that the community resources are so used as to subserve the common good. Moreover, it is now asserted that that the command or ownership of the community are non-negotiable. A person can best assume the role of a manager but the resource vests in the community.

Former President of India, Dr. K.R. Narayanan, while inaugurating conference organized by the Centre for Science and Environment on 'Potential of Water Harvesting' at New Delhi, warned the nation on 3 October 1998: "This (water) universal asset is being fast depleted. Leading experts on water resources have been warning that the world is heading towards a 'water shock' which may dwarf the oil crisis. Some 80 countries and 40 per cent of the world's population are already experiencing 'water stress'. Environmental degradation and population explosion are making the problem even more acute, with pollution poisoning the water that is available."

Need for the Community Involvement

Former President of India, Dr. K.R. Narayanan stressed upon people's participation emphasizing that "India today needs a people's movement to meet its water needs and to protect its water sources. We must get every community involved both in the provision of water and in the protection of water sources. Civil society has to play a critical role in encouraging equity and sustainability in the use of water". Increase in human and bovine population of the country has resulted not only in reduction of per capita availability of net area cultivated but also in substantial reduction in availability of common properties for grazing for the cattle and shortage of fuel wood for domestic purposes. There have also been increasing number of cases of grabbing of common lands by influential people of the villages. In earlier years after independence, the pressure on lands was not so much, because there was enough land available for people as well as cattle, nobody thought of reclaiming waste lands or conserving flowing waters, but after increased demand for agriculture and diminishing water levels, need for management of natural resources has become imminent. The present status of management of forests, land and water is a big question mark since environment is degrading fast in spite of the best efforts of the government, and biomass is almost disappearing not only from the pastures but also from reserved forests, what to talk of unreserved forests. Hence, it is already high time that the community should come forward to protect common property resources to save it from the shackles of unscrupulous hands in the common interest. Community should come forward boldly for management of natural resources to get maximum and purposeful returns from land, water and forest.

In such a historical process, the role of government should evolve from that of being a system manager to that of being a service provider. Farmers should move from water recipients to water users and then as water co-managers along with irrigation department. But this is not an easy process for agencies to accommodate beneficiaries and make space for so-called reserved domain of administration. There can be many ups and downs in performance and examples of success and failures may be there. But participation is essential in view of prevailing conditions specially when it is not possible for the state to maintain the irrigation as well as drinking water infrastructure due to financial constraints. This is true not only of India but other countries in the world also. It is now felt that one of the most important reason for these problems is lack of stakeholders' participation in water management.

Integrated Effort of Participatory Water Management

Participatory management of water may not be panacea for all water management issues, but yet it can go a long way in ensuring efficient running of canals, optimum on-field water application and proper drainage of excess water from irrigation systems and farmers' fields. Such participatory management can work only if all the stakeholders, farmers, irrigation agency employees including engineers, government, etc., feel that participatory management will further their individual and group or community interests, both singly and jointly. Farmers should feel an urge to come together in water user associations and to take over water management functions. Government employees should realize the need to change their ways. Training and orientation of both farmers as well as irrigation or other water agencies is needed for preparing all the stakeholders for success of participatory management.

The Rajiv Gandhi Foundation Drinking Water Mission along with donor agencies also gave priority to community-based drinking water supply schemes. 'Sector reform' project was initiated in 55 districts of India including four districts of Alwar, Sikar, Rajsamand and Jaipur (Rajasthan) in the first instance some four years ago. Since 26 January 2003, it has been started in all the districts under the new nomenclature of 'Swajaldhara'. The scheme envisages 10 per cent contribution by the community and complete planning, execution and management of the water supply scheme by the rural community.

Thus, community management is becoming increasingly pertinent in the management of common property resources. Though ownership and management of these resources rested with the State for a long time, the government's failure to preserve common property resources together with their excessive exploitation for development has led to serious degradation of the environment with the attendant ecological repercussions. Under people's participation as an alternative, the beneficiaries are made responsive to the cost of preservation. Such a system makes development with preservation possible.

Successful Experiments

There have been many successful experiments of community management of water resources. But all these success stories prove that community alone cannot achieve results unless some devoted social activists form a group of sincere workers who work incessantly in rural area with missionary zeal. Motivation, guidance, training and support to community in the form of technical and financial assistance combined with involvement of local community and help and assistance by concerned government departments can create successful examples.

Real Objective

Community participation in water management should be genuine partnership between farmers and the government as a whole and not merely as an instrument for facilitating government schemes and programmes. Solving fiscal problem is not the goal. Farmer's direct involvement in system management as a compliment/substitute to state's role should be the basic objective. It is not privatization which refers to transfer of ownership to the agency but direct and effective involvement of beneficiaries in decision-making process.

From Participation to Management

The idea that the farmers should 'participate' in irrigation management has grown in India since 1980s, though formally adopted in National Water Policy, 1987 and Eighth Plan. Irrigation projects proved a disguised boon only. People's participation was fervently advocated by many sections of society. Bureaucrats saw possible benefits in probable reduction in operating costs, lightening their burden of maintenance, collection of water charges, etc. Farmer's perspective is satisfaction of his genuine need for irrigating his fields. He wants equity in distribution of water if it is scarce, specially at the tail end. WUAs are to be used to develop them as a power base and to empower the community to take over management of water resources. It should come from below and not be imposed from above if people have to manage and be really empowered to take over operation and maintenance of the system. Participation is only advisory where decision-making power rests with the agency and not with the users. Hence, it is 'management' and not 'participation' which can really deliver the goods. Farmers are the chief clients who can take initiative for irrigation assessment, planning, management, equitable water distribution, collection of water charges, maintenance, etc. Farmers are not only the beneficiaries but the managers of the product (water) which they purchase and for which they pay to the supplier and be accountable. There should be no paternalistic attitude.

The experience of various states indicates that Kuhls as managed by community in Himachal Pradesh, tubewells in west Bengal or Uttar Pradesh, tanks in Tamil Nadu, were of course successful. In pilot projects also, there was initial success but community management on sustainable basis is yet an exception. A climate is yet to be built for changing the mindset of irrigation officials. Community organizers have to create an initiative and build capacity among farmers to take over management of irrigation systems in times to come. Legal enactments alone as passed by different states may not be the way forward.

Watershed Projects

Since most of the lands specially of the poor and marginalized farmers are rainfed, they have to depend on rains. That is why, due to erratic rains, Indian agriculture is said to be 'a gamble in rains'. Moreover, more than 70 per cent rain water is said to be wasted in rivers and nallas. Community has to be involved for rain water conservation also. Necessarily watershed development projects will also have to be planned, implemented and maintained through active and willing participation of the people. There will be community participation in soil and water management only when they perceive direct and tangible benefits for themselves and understand technology. The full participation of the watershed committees may be facilitated when the programme is built up on their accumulated wisdom, skills and systems. The complicated technologies imposed from outside inhibit willing participation of the local people. Instead of government projects with people's participation, they should be people's projects with government participation.

People's participation has to be ensured throughout the project cycle.

New approach of participatory natural resource management would enthuse the people, make the development programmes really useful for the local people, and make them come forward to welcome and participate in the great national venture towards sustainable management of the natural resources to produce abundance for our growing population without damaging the resource base.

Community Pumpsets

To give irrigation facility to marginal and small farmers in tribal areas, a group of 3-5 small or marginal farmers owning a well or a water source of river/nalla/tank/anicut nearer the land to be irrigated are given pumpset free of cost to be run on participative basis. About 15-20 groups are benefited every year. Maintenance of pump set is responsibility of group members. There is also a chairman and secretary of the group.

Lift Irrigation Schemes

As regards community participation in lift irrigation schemes, it was revealed that cultivator beneficiaries became ready to contribute their 10 per cent share only after 10-15 extension meetings. Though community was enthusiastic in the beginning but it could not own the scheme. They continued to treat it as a government scheme and found faults with it rather than running it successfully to their advantage. Some of the members defaulted in payment of their share of electricity dues or digging their canals or fixing outlet pipes. Default of few members resulted in whole community to suffer due to non-cooperation in the scheme.

Beneficiaries were well aware of the need for irrigation and they were eager to get the benefits but with minimum or no public contribution. Individual selfishness is more dominant than community feeling. Enthusiasm shown by the farmers at initial stage does not subsist long due to inter-member disputes due to shortage of power supply for irrigation of crops. They suggested that irresponsible members should not be included in the project to avoid disconnection for non-payment. Cultivators should not let loose their cattle so as to damage the crop raised by few farmers. Proper technical guidance should be continued as follow up by RSEB and DRDA officials for successful running of the schemes after initial commissioning. There were few ideal examples also where lift irrigation projects have been successfully running due to full cooperation of members.

Thus, it is clear from the analysis of the constraints identified in successful implementation of minor irrigation, that active involvement and participation of the people is yet to take a concrete shape and form a movement. This calls for evolving a definite multi-pronged strategy which may encompass awareness generation, resource mobilization and sustainable interest and enthusiasm as its key components. Needless to say that PRIs alone are capable of taking care of this strategy and ensuring its proper follow-up in the field. They can rely upon necessary support of official and voluntary agencies in their mission for rural development, and upon people by imparting and cultivating a proper outlook among the beneficiaries who are still illiterate, poor and backward. It will be with a missionary mission alone that the dream of Bapu's Gram Swarajya can be realized.

Community Tubewells

Surface water has been managed by community through tank irrigation in the states of Karnataka and Andhra Pradesh since times immemorial but groundwater management through community is of recent origin. In Uttar Pradesh, World Bank aided public tubewells (PTWs) were designed with superior technology. Field water distributaries and feeders were dug. Electricity was assured for 16-18 hours. Agricultural extension service was also dovetailed with it. Farmers were involved in water distribution systems. PTWs are meant to benefit the marginal and poorer farmers. Tubewells are in clusters of 25 each, in areas where economically backward people reside. The pattern of water distribution reflects the extent of farmers' participation in management of water resources from PTWs. Provision for farmers' participation was made at the layout stage itself. Benefits were quite gratifying.

In West Bengal also, many tubewells were turned over to panchayats. The panchayats, in turn, have turned them over to the user groups for actual management, though the accounting is under the supervision of the panchayats. This is said to be successful. Groups of farmers instal pumpsets, and sell the water a little cheaper than the market rate. Though these are nominally supervised by panchayat but each group works independently.

In north Gujarat also, entrepreneur farmers get together and invest in tubewells, each of which irrigates 100-150 acres. Surplus water not required by members is sold out at Rs. 18 an hour. There is a water market and sometimes a farmer has a choice of getting water from several outlets near his land. Another alternative model in Gujarat is that of tubewell companies. From 5 to 120 members having landholding in the command form an informal organization which is not registered. All promoters of the company enter into an agreement and elect a manager, open a bank account and all resources are internally generated. There is complete autonomy and self governance. They run tubewells on community basis.

Need for Change in Drinking Water Policy

The strategies of rural water supply programme hitherto adopted revolved around the basic premise that provision of safe drinking water is the responsibility of the government. A change in the technology focus to hand pumps fitted on tubewells and borewells had resulted in an impressive increase in total rural water supply coverage. However, the availability of potable drinking water in rural area, specially during the summer months, is still not satisfactory. Even though about one lakh habitations are covered every year, the number of problem habitations has not declined proportionately. Fast depletion of groundwater level, heavy emphasis on new construction and poor attention to maintenance, non-involvement of people in operations and maintenance, neglect of traditional water management practices created a necessity to involve community in drinking water management also so as to cover all rural habitations and reach the unreached with access to safe drinking water. Experience has shown that wherever women are involved in such consultation and in maintenance of the sources, the performance of supply systems has been effective.

In Rajasthan, 'Aapni Yojna' being implemented in district Churu with German aid is exemplary as a community drinking water scheme. It is water democracy in action. It is a global rural water supply project of unusual size and complexity. It is implemented by the community with the help of NGO partners under the guidance of German consultants. Sustainable supply of water is ensured from Indira Gandhi Canal. Public stand posts and cattle water troughs are constructed in villages as part of the project. Framework of participation is at various levels. An important participation bond is between the project staff and the community. The regular interaction of CPU field staff with community has developed trust among the community for this project. The field intervention has empowered the village level community for managing their internal system independently. The communities are enthusiastically participating in all activities of the project.

Women's empowerment is there with full community participation. Aapni Yojna is the first of its kind in the desert area.

On the similar pattern are being implemented the sector reforms and swajaldhara project from April 1999 in rural water supply sector for institutionalizing community participation. It was mainly because water is today perceived by the rural public as a social right, to be provided free by the government, rather than as a scarce resource which must be managed locally as a socio-economic good in order to ensure its effective use. New policy is a transformation from a target-based, supply-driven approach which pays little attention to preferences of end-users, to a demand-based approach where users get the service they want and are willing to pay for is urgently required. Implementation of a participatory demand-driven approach will ensure that the public obtain the level of service they desire and can afford to pay. During review of sector reform projects, the experience of community participation was not very much encouraging as only 29 per cent schemes could be completed and 24 per cent were handed over to community for running and maintenance.

Participatory and community-led 'Swajaldhara' is the latest experiment in community management of drinking water programme which was launched as a reform initiative throughout the country from 25 December 2002. United Nations General Assembly also declared year 2003 the 'International Year of Fresh Water'. The role of governments has to shift from service provider to that of facilitator for providing financial and policy support to the communities and their institutions for fulfilling the desired levels of services on a sustainable and equitable basis. There is increasing awareness of the need to strengthen technical and managerial capacity of different tiers of local governments.

There is global consensus that "management at the lowest appropriate level" is an important prerequisite for sustainability. The strategy has changed from the top-down, fully government implemented approach in Maharashtra to a community participation approach to Karnataka through a "demand responsive approach in partnership with NGOs and User Groups" in Uttar Pradesh, and finally to "Community driven development" in Kerala and Karnataka. The World Bank-assisted Rural Water Supply and Sanitation Project (popularly known as Swajal (pure water) in Uttar Pradesh has been acknowledged nationally and internationally as the best practice example in implementing a demand responsive approach.

Ground Reality

Due to age long practice of spoon feeding the villagers since independence, it will take a very long time to bring attitudinal change in mindset of people living in rural areas. Departmental hold on contractors and traders will hardly allow village level committees to implement schemes independently. Moreover, technical dependence on PHED engineers for preparing project and ensuring quality material as well as proper maintenance will still continue in view of limited capacity building of village level committees. Voluntary work of collection of water charges and account keeping by villagers independently may result in more failures than success. Panchayats are also not equipped with competent staff to take over O&M responsibilities. Community management of water has successes to its credit but in special cases as in Churu, Indo-German Drinking Water Project (Rajasthan). In watershed development, Sukho Majri experience of Haryana, Peepalwas and Losing Watershed projects (Udaipur), Ralegaon Sidhi of Maharashtra are leading examples of community management. Similarly, in forests, Chipko forest movement of Himachal Pradesh, Rangabelia flood protection and rural development project of Sundarbans and Arabari joint forest management committee of West Bengal, Vankar forest cooperatives in Gujarat and forest cooperatives of Uttranchal, Purulia and Community Dug Well Irrigation Scheme in village Samraspur of Cuttack, Orissa, Pani Panchayats of Pune district, Johad's watersheds and Arvari river rejuvenation by Tarun Bharat Sangh in Thana Ghazi (Alwar) are on the national map as exemplary cases of community management of water and other natural resources.

Hence, it is essential that bureaucrats change their attitude of acting as facilitators for the community. Sincere efforts are required to build the capacity of user committees to shoulder the responsibility of management. NGOs will have to come forward to act as catalyst for empowering the stakeholders to manage community resources. Government will have to facilitate it through appropriate changes in rules and procedures and encourage NGOs for necessary interventions for the desired change. Leadership at the community level will also prove helpful in such paradigm shift.

Index